I0748866

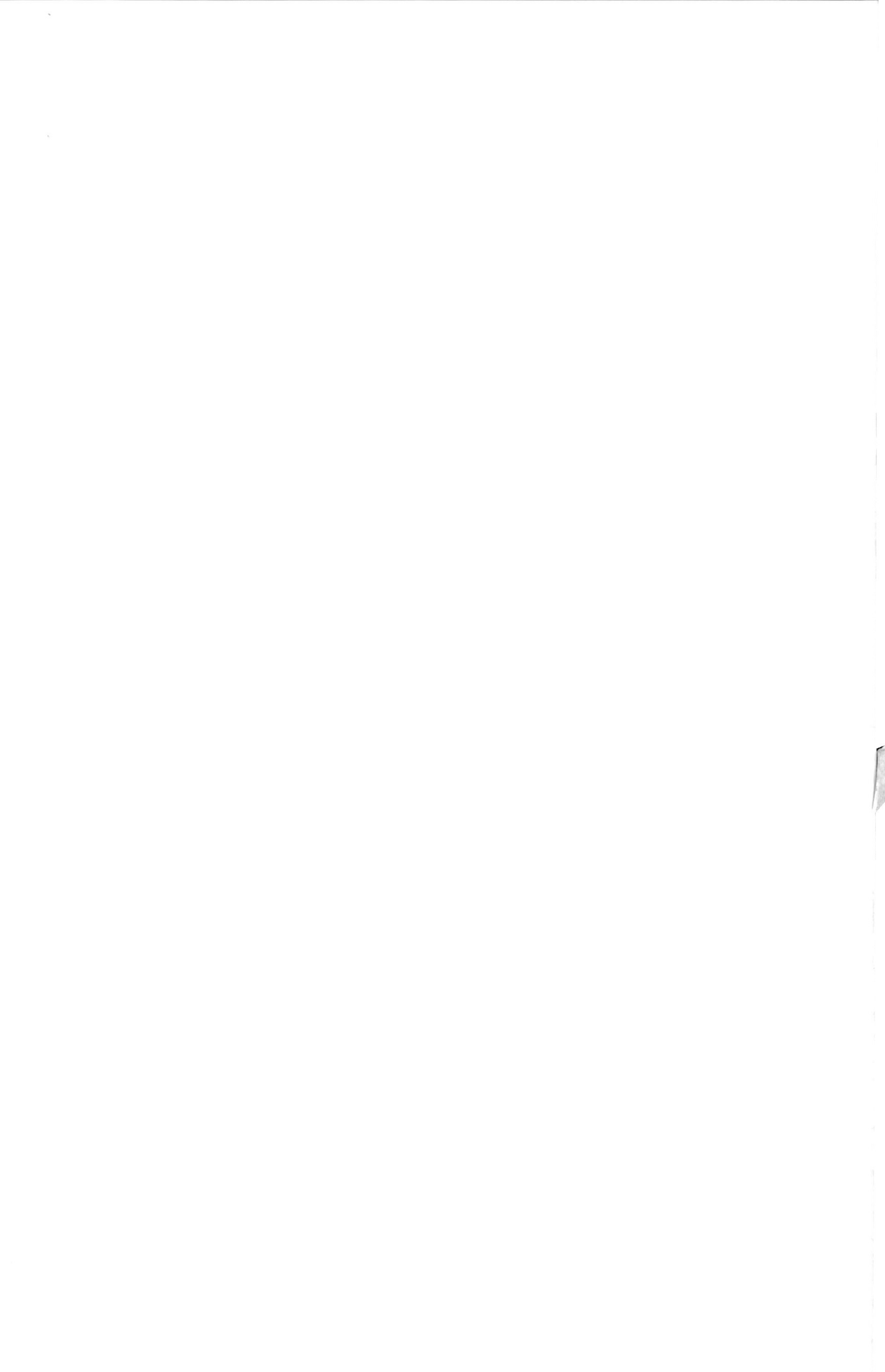

A Portrait
OF
Elizabeth Willing Powel

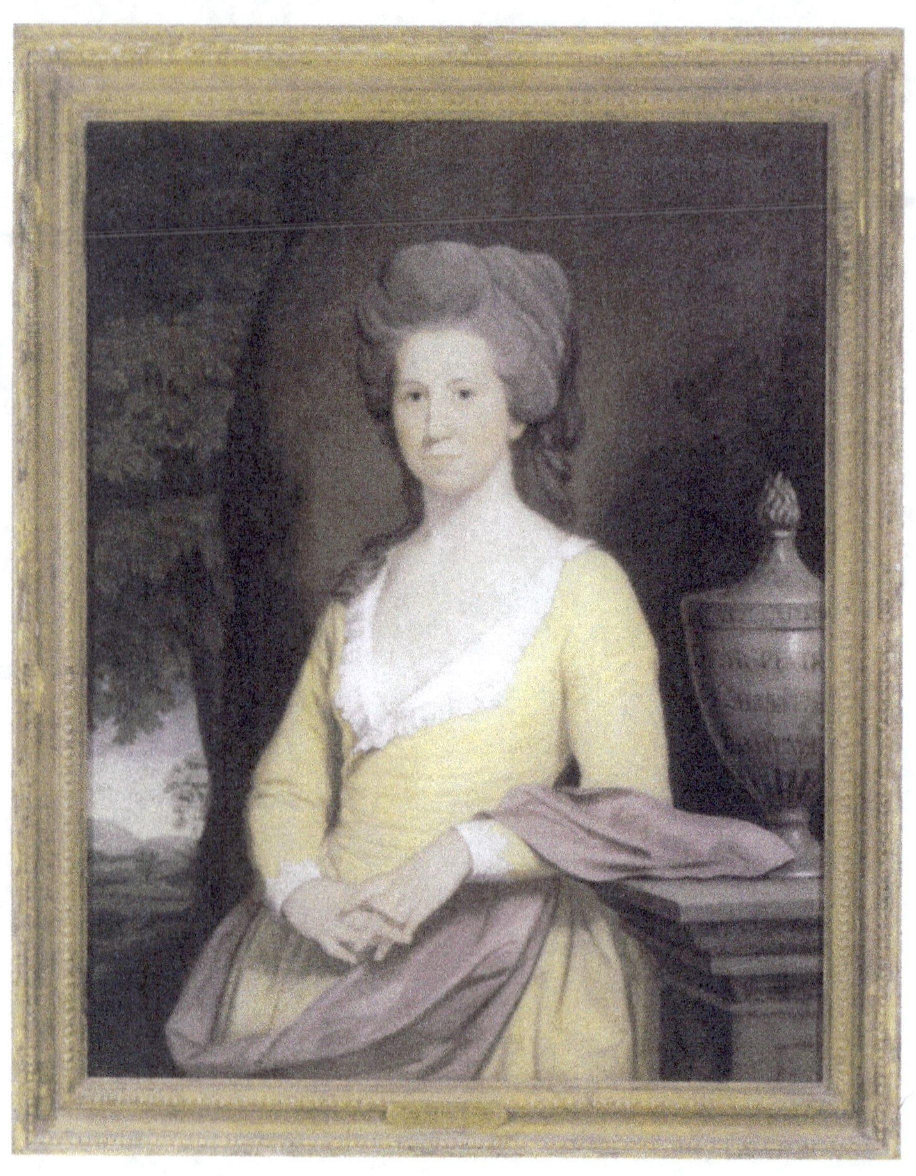

A Portrait
OF
Elizabeth Willing Powel
(1743–1830)

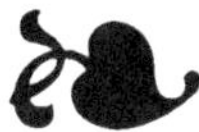

David W. Maxey

American Philosophical Society
Philadelphia • 2006

Transactions of the
American Philosophical Society
Held at Philadelphia
For Promoting Useful Knowledge
Volume 96, Part 4

Library of Congress Cataloging-in-Publication Data

Maxey, David W. (David Walker), 1934-
A portrait of Elizabeth Willing Powel (1743-1830) / David W. Maxey.
p. cm. – (Transactions of the American Philosophical Society ; v. 96, pt. 4)
Includes bibliographical references and index.
ISBN-13: 978-0-87169-964-0
ISBN-10: 0-87169-964-8 (pbk.)
1. Powel, Elizabeth Willing, 1743-1830. 2. Powel, Elizabeth Willing, 1743-1830—Portraits. 3. Politicians' spouses—Pennsylvania—Philadelphia—Biography. 4. Politicians' spouses—Pennsylvania—Philadelphia—Portraits. 5. Philadelphia (Pa.)—Social life and customs—18th century. 6. Pratt, Matthew, 1734-1805. Elizabeth Willing Powel. 7. Philadelphia (Pa.)—Biography. 8. Powel, Elizabeth Willing, 1743-1830—Family. 9. Powell family. I. Title. II. Series.

F158.54.P68 M39 2006
974.8'1102092—dc22
[B] 2006045853

For Cath

O well wept, mother have lost son;
Wept, wife; wept, sweetheart would be one:
  Though grief yield them no good
Yet shed what tears sad truelove should.

—Gerard Manley Hopkins, *The Loss of the Eurydice*

Contents

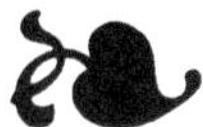

List of Illustrations

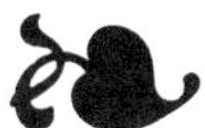

Preface

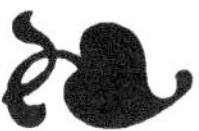

THE POWEL HOUSE IS A PRECIOUS REMNANT of Philadelphia's eighteenth-century past. Through sometimes hazardous passage, it has arrived in the safe custody of the Philadelphia Society for the Preservation of Landmarks.

To qualify as a guide at the Powel House, one must assimilate a considerable body of historical fact and interpretation. Inevitably, however, there are questions thoughtful visitors ask that cannot be easily answered. As an occasional guide at the Powel House, I have faltered more than once in my response when confronted with Matthew Pratt's portrait of Elizabeth Powel. Only in a superficial sense may that portrait and its subject be regarded as revealing.

What follows in these pages is an attempt to unlock the secrets of the painting's composition and subsequent history, while presenting a more extended view of a woman who, when seen in context two centuries ago, continues to merit our attention and respect. Aware that Elizabeth Powel cared lifelong about the image she presented, I would like to think that she might accept this slender volume as sympathetic portraiture—and no less so because it seeks to be revealing.

I am grateful for various assistance I have received from successive managers at the Powel House, Laurie C. Switzer, Michele Herr, J. Del Conner, Michelle Wilson and Robert Wuilfe, and also from Carol E. Soltis, the Philadelphia Museum of Art; Leslie Hunt, The Historical Society of Pennsylvania; Whitfield J. Bell, Jr., Mary C. McDonald, and Frank Margeson, American Philosophical Society; Mary V. Thompson and Barbara McMillan, Mount Vernon Ladies' Association; Linda Baumgarten, Colonial Williamsburg Foundation; Cheryl Leibold, Gale Rawson, and Barbara Katus, The Pennsylvania Academy of the Fine Arts; Phillip Lapsansky, The Library Company of Philadelphia; John Rhodehamel, Huntington Library; Becky Cape, The Lilly Library, Indiana University; and Anne Verplanck, Winterthur Museum. I am particularly indebted to the anonymous reviewer of my manuscript who provided many helpful comments and suggestions.

1

An Enigmatic Portrait

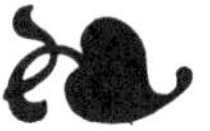

SHE GAZES OUT IMPASSIVELY across the divide of more than two centuries, inviting us to decipher the coded message her portrait contains. No classic beauty, she appears in a strange setting and in clothing not easily labeled. From beneath a beehive of lightly powdered hair, her facial expression conveys a sense of muted sadness.

The portrait's dimensions and elements of formal composition suggest that it represented an important commission, such that the artist who painted it would have been expected to do right by his client and her wishes. His subject, wearing a low-cut yellow dress, seems free of the constraint that stays typically imposed in portraiture of women of a certain age in the late eighteenth century.[1] The dress's long tight sleeves taper to sawtooth cuffs, drawing attention to the fingers of the sitter's hands, which are interlaced in a pattern that may provide a clue to the painting's hidden meaning. A purple scarf is draped across her body. To reinforce the somber effect, the woman in the yellow dress has avoided wearing any jewelry. On a pedestal to her left stands a funerary urn whose inscription, in the canvas's darkened condition, is now barely legible: "Dear Pledg/ of Chaste &/Farewe." In the immediate background looms a rock formation, and in the far distance, on the low horizon to the sitter's right, are trees, a meadow, and hills.[2]

How else can one interpret this enigmatic portrait except as the picture of a woman in mourning? If the dress she wears and its design are to all appearances unstaid, there is nevertheless no mistaking the urn with its fragmentary inscription and the purple scarf as symbols of grief.[3] Today the painting, on generous loan from the Pennsylvania Academy of the Fine Arts, hangs in the rear second-floor drawing room of that elegant mid-Georgian structure located on Third Street in Philadelphia known as the Powel House. By general agreement it is now accepted as the work of the Philadelphia artist Matthew Pratt, depicting Elizabeth Willing Powel. Because her husband, Samuel Powel, died in 1793, a victim of the yellow fever epidemic that ravaged Philadelphia in the late summer and early fall of that year, it is also frequently assumed that the portrait shows Mrs. Powel in mourning for him.[4]

Elizabeth Powel remained a widow for thirty-six years, dying on January 17, 1830. Her funeral service five days later was both a social event and a religious experience. It was presided over by her friend and a coexecutor she named under her will, the venerable Bishop William White. The ceremony was conducted, Deborah Norris Logan noted approvingly in her diary, "in the old fashioned manner: The Corpse borne on Men's shoulders and covered with a Pall was followed by Relations and friends and domestics, and then by Citizens. About four and twenty Coaches attended."

A scrupulous Quaker, Deborah Logan was not among the guests in attendance at the funeral, although her relatives assured her that an invitation meant for her had unaccountably gone astray. Her feelings about Elizabeth

Powel, almost twenty years her senior whom she had observed at a distance for a long time, were ambivalent. While she conceded that she was "a talented woman, always, I believe, just and honourable in her dealings and often generous to others," she found her attachment to the things of this world unedifying. The ambivalence Logan felt may be traced to Samuel Powel's peremptory defection from the Society of Friends and the eventual transfer of his inherited wealth to his wife's family. Logan regarded as an instructive lesson what friends reported of a dinner conversation with Elizabeth Powel a month before the older woman died. They described her in "an affecting state of nervous irritability and mental distress," exclaiming " 'Have I ever done good in my life? Can people go to Heaven without doing good?' "[5]

Elizabeth Powel was buried next to her husband in the Christ Church graveyard at Fifth and Arch Streets. In a last attempt at self-portrayal, the inscription on her tombstone pays tribute to her "good sense and good works." Though clearly how in the end she wished to be remembered, the terse epitaph she chose for herself fails to do justice to the influential position she occupied in a well-connected family, in the upper reaches of Philadelphia society, and indeed in the history of this nation at its infancy.[6]

This mysterious painting attributed to Matthew Pratt must therefore be placed in a larger framework to determine how faithfully it captures its subject and delivers the particular message she intended. That an extensive record is available to assist in such an inquiry is due, in no small part, to Elizabeth Powel's appreciation of the role she played and the merits she possessed. In clear, bold handwriting she meticulously made copies of the letters she sent to a wide range of relatives, friends, and acquaintances—all of the letters ending (including the copies) with the hallmark signature of "Eliza Powel." The flow of correspondence would continue until the beginning of the 1820s when old age, painful rheumatism, and failing eyesight deprive us of the privileged view we have of her through these letters.[7]

The dating, provenance, and interpretation of the Pratt portrait have remained problematic. This study will endeavor to shed light on these issues, while at the same time providing greater access to the personality and style of a woman of discerning intelligence and strong opinions.

2

The Academy's Acquisition of the Portrait and Its Attribution to Matthew Pratt

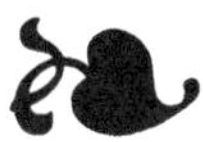

THE PAINTING HAS BEEN IN THE collections of the Pennsylvania Academy of the Fine Arts since 1912. In that year the academy acquired it from a Philadelphia dealer, Robert M. Lindsay, who had offered the painting for sale as the work first of Charles Willson Peale and then of John Singleton Copley. On the understanding that it was indeed a Copley, but with no supporting provenance furnished by Lindsay, the academy's board authorized the purchase of the portrait for an expenditure of as much as eight hundred dollars. As luck would have it, the academy wound up buying the painting at the knockdown price of six hundred and seventy-five dollars.[8]

The Copley attribution was almost immediately challenged. In 1915 the editor of *American Art News*, lamenting the inadequacy of an exhibition of early American painters, cited as an example "the one Copley shown," this portrait that the academy had recently acquired, which he suggested had to be "seriously questioned." Little wonder, thundered an outspoken art critic and historian in a letter printed in the next issue of that publication:

> Any tyro in American art would know that this canvas was not painted by John Singleton Copley. It has no relation whatever to his work, was assuredly painted after 1774, when Copley left the country, and is as certainly the work of James Peale as any unsigned canvas can be attributed to any painter. The institution that purchased this portrait for a small price, after it had been repeatedly turned down as a Copley, even if it is willing to fool itself into the idea that it is what it is not, has no right to attempt to fool others into following its folly.[9]

The source of this pointed attack was Charles Henry Hart. A member of the academy's board from 1882 to 1902 and the organizer, to his credit, of a pathbreaking exhibition at the academy in the winter of 1887–1888, Hart had abandoned his profitable career as a Philadelphia lawyer to become the self-appointed arbiter of suspect attributions in early American portraiture, of which, happily from his standpoint, there were many. Nothing thrilled him more than exposing spuriously labeled canvases in language that often caused vulnerable curators to wince. During this second career, he fired off countless letters to the editor and published essays and monographs by the score. In these rulings he so confidently made, he ran the inevitable risk of being flat-out wrong; worse yet, for personal gain, he became implicated in knowingly erroneous attributions.[10]

For thirty years the academy stuck to its guns and continued to catalogue the portrait as a Copley. Then, in 1942, the director of the New-York Historical Society sought permission to include the painting as an illustration in a monograph the society was about to publish. The author of the monograph, William Sawitzky, had determined in a comprehensive survey of a number of canvases of questionable attribution that the portrait was the handiwork of the Philadelphia limner and sign-painter Matthew Pratt (1734–1805); Sawitzky also assigned it the date "circa 1793." Though eventually consenting to the request, the academy's secretary replied that the attribution to Pratt came as "news to us." He added, "At the present time, and indeed since the purchase of the picture, the attribution has read 'John S. Copley.' "[11]

Sawitzky reached his conclusions based less on historical evidence concerning Pratt and his patrons than on common characteristics he identified in the artist's oeuvre—such as the mixed hues in Pratt's palette, the tendency noticeable in his later portraits toward opaque and even dull coloring, the awkward modeling of faces, the idiosyncratic treatment of his subjects' eyes, and a peculiar failure to render hands in other than a clumsy fashion. Sawitzky labored under more than one handicap, however, in attempting to establish what Pratt indisputably produced.[12]

With but a single known exception, Pratt did not sign or date his portraits. Nor, during his most productive period as a portrait painter, did he stay put in any one place, catering to an identifiable clientele.[13] Though born, raised, and initially trained in Philadelphia, and though he married and obtained his first commissions there, Pratt was for many years, if not, technically speaking, an itinerant painter, certainly a restless one. In 1755, after having served an apprenticeship with his uncle James Claypoole as "Limner and Painter in general," he set out on his own in that occupation. He changed course for a year and embarked on a trading expedition to Jamaica. This venture came to an abrupt and painful end when the ship on which he sailed as supercargo was seized within a matter of days by a French and then by a Jamaican privateer. Chastened, Pratt returned to Philadelphia in May 1758 to begin the practice of portrait painting in earnest. He soon could congratulate himself on "making money fast, with the approbation of every employer," and in August 1760 he married Elizabeth Moore.[14]

He left Philadelphia again in June 1764 in the company of his cousin Betsy Shewell and John West, the father of Benjamin West. Betsy Shewell and Benjamin West had been engaged since 1760 when West had gone abroad to expand his artistic horizons and eventually to make his reputation in Britain as a celebrated painter of neoclassical and realistic historical canvases. A few weeks after arriving in England, Pratt had the pleasant duty of giving the bride away at a wedding ceremony performed at St. Martin's in the Strand. Joining the newlyweds on their honeymoon, Pratt moved in afterwards as their boarder and spent the next eighteen months perfecting his technique in West's studio. Pratt later recorded in an autobiographical note that although his junior by several years, West treated him during this stay "as if I was his Father, friend and brother." While thus employed, Pratt painted the canvas by which he is best known, a group portrait showing West giving instruction to his pupils, one of whom is Matthew Pratt. *The American School*, now at the Metropolitan

Museum of Art, is the only extant painting of Pratt's that is signed and dated. At the end of his apprenticeship with West, Pratt went on to Bristol, where he wrote that he "practiced to much advantage, in my professional line."[15]

Eventually making his way back to Philadelphia in 1768, Pratt crossed the Atlantic less than two years later. This time his mission was to claim a legacy due his wife in the care of a churchman in Ireland. While abroad for a mere three months in the spring of 1770, he nevertheless found the opportunity to paint several portraits in Ireland and in England. After another short interval in Philadelphia, he set up shop briefly in New York and later in Williamsburg. During the spring of 1773, he placed successive advertisements in the *Virginia Gazette*, first offering for sale from an inventory of canvases in his possession copies he had made of famous paintings while he was abroad, then announcing his intention to leave Williamsburg for Jamaica, and finally giving notice of his decision to linger in Virginia during the summer months while he looked for commissions.[16] The Revolutionary War period was presumably not a good time for a portrait painter to practice his trade in America, and Pratt, not surprisingly, drops out of sight. His wife, from whom he was often separated during the years of their marriage, died in 1777 and was buried in the family plot in the Christ Church graveyard at Fifth and Arch Streets.[17]

Pratt surfaced once more after the war was over. In the first Philadelphia city directory of 1785, he is listed at his address on Pine Street between Second and Third as "Portrait & Sign Painter."[18] Although in newspaper advertisements he continued to present himself as a portrait painter, he had begun to shift to sign painting as the principal source of his income. In explaining this change of direction, his son Thomas would later write, "I think about 1785 the Fine arts, were very poorly encouraged in Philad[elphi]a and during which time, my Father, having little to do in that Line, was prevailed upon, by a number of particular friends, to paint some signs, and he consented thereto." Unfortunately, none of the signs has survived that he painted for tradesmen and tavern keepers at various locations in Philadelphia, often accompanied by legends in verse of Pratt's improvising; by all accounts, however, his work was admired as having been carried out with panache. Although there are portraits painted after the Revolution that can be reliably attributed to Pratt, this had clearly become for him a secondary calling.[19]

Upon his return to Philadelphia in 1768, Pratt persuaded a good friend, the Reverend Thomas Barton of Lancaster, to travel to the city for the purpose of supplying introductions "to Governor Hamilton, Governor Johnson, Mr. Jno Dickinson, Mr. Saml Powel, and all the Willing family, the Clergy &tc &tc." Barton was more than just a country parson; the patron and brother-in-law of David Rittenhouse and the father of the physician and botanist Benjamin Smith Barton, he later refused to take the oath of allegiance and fled as a loyalist to New York, where he died in 1780.[20] From these well-placed members of Philadelphia society to whom Barton introduced him, Pratt obtained commissions that kept him busy for the two years he stayed in Philadelphia before leaving for Ireland.

It was in that period that Pratt painted his first portrait of Elizabeth Willing, who was either just married or on the verge of being so. In Pratt's portrayal of her, we see a person of sober mien who, if reconciled to the married state, is hardly brimming over with happiness (Figure 1).[21] The portrait does serve, however, to authenticate the one that is the principal focus of this study. The woman in the yellow dress has the same sharp features, albeit softened with the passage of time, the same high forehead, the same prominent nose, the same slightly receding chin, and the same tress of hair hanging over her right shoulder. It must be said that such commitment to verisimilitude did not dissuade another Willing sister from sitting a few years later for her portrait by Pratt. When he was in Virginia in 1773, trying to find commissions, he painted Mary Byrd. And in this case, there is also no mistaking that two sisters who looked alike had sat for the same artist.[22]

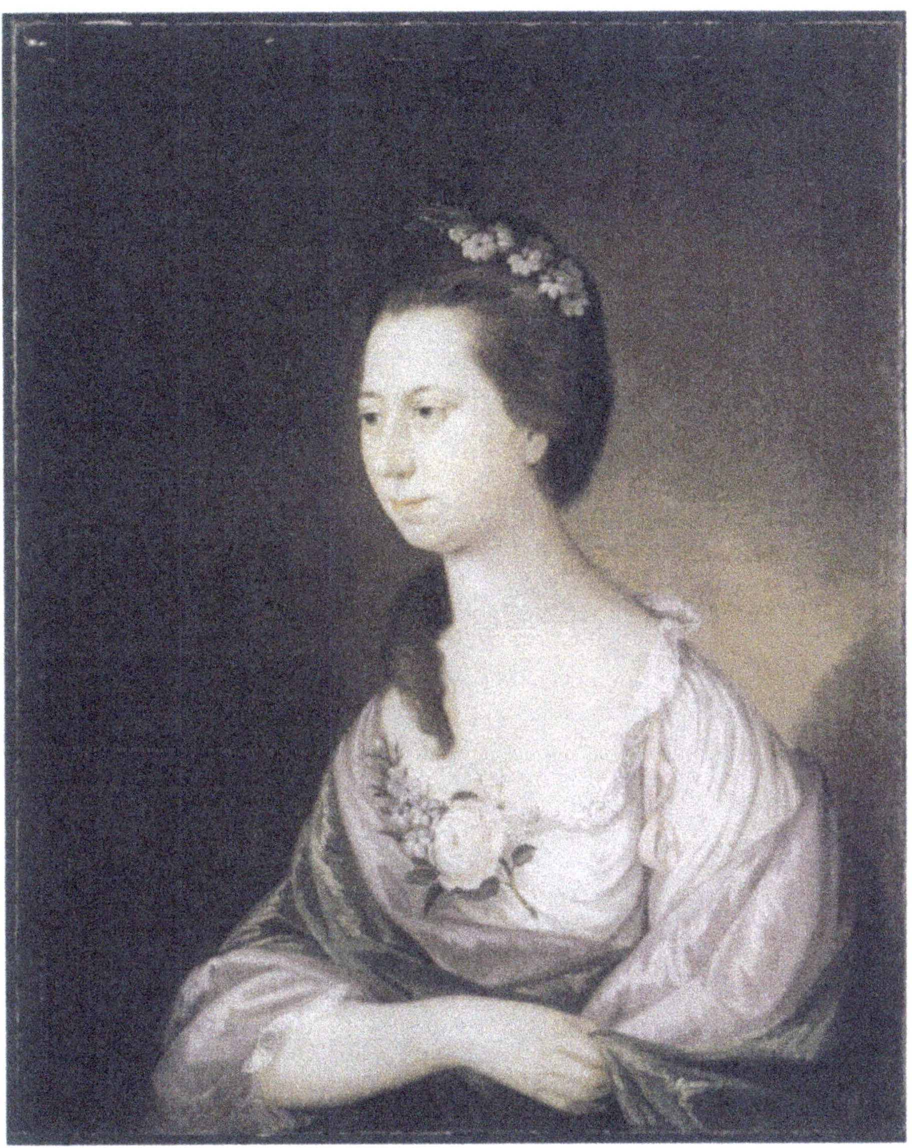

FIGURE 1. Portrait of Elizabeth Willing Powel, attributed to Matthew Pratt and painted in 1768–1769, at about the time of her marriage to Samuel Powel. Courtesy of the Philadelphia Museum of Art.

3

The Subject of the Portrait Viewed in Enlarged Perspective

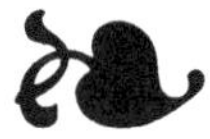

WHAT DO THE TWO PORTRAITS OF Elizabeth Willing Powel, and especially the later one, reveal of its subject, of her true feelings and aspirations, of the reason why she may have chosen at that time in her life to leave a visual record of herself? "[H]aving one's portrait taken in the eighteenth century," an expert appraiser has written, "was not a matter to be taken lightly . . . [for] portraits did not come cheap, and required a considerable investment of time on the part of both sitter and artist."[23] Moreover, the reciprocal responsibilities of the two parties to this exercise could be described as daunting. In *An Essay on the Theory of Painting* (1715), a volume that Benjamin West owned when Pratt was his student in London, Jonathan Richardson laid it down that "to sit for one's picture is to have an Abstract of one's Life written, and published, and ourselves thus consign'd over to Honour, or Infamy."[24] How many applied for their portraits with such exposure clearly in mind is a question one may well pause over, and yet motivation had to exist if only to provide a likeness to be remembered by. The Willing family, both in Elizabeth Powel's generation and before, recurrently sought this opportunity as we know from several available canvases recording images of its members.[25]

Elizabeth Powel's father, Charles Willing, was born in Bristol, England, in 1710, the son of Thomas Willing, a prosperous merchant, and Anne Harrison Willing. This grandmother of Elizabeth Powel was in her turn the granddaughter of Thomas Harrison and of Simon Mayne, members of the Long Parliament who signed the death warrant of Charles I. At the Restoration, Thomas Harrison, as an unrepentant regicide, was sentenced to be hanged, drawn, and quartered. He went forward to meet that gruesome fate with remarkable serenity, proclaiming to the very end his attachment to the "Good Old Cause." From such hardy stock Elizabeth Powel could claim descent on her father's side.[26]

Her maternal inheritance was less heroic. Her great-grandfather Edward Shippen left England for Boston in 1669 at about thirty years of age. After arriving in Massachusetts, he married Elizabeth Lybrand, a Quaker, and soon became a member of the Society of Friends by convincement. For these newly acquired religious convictions he received a public whipping. With the subsidence of Puritan persecution, he would eventually prosper as a merchant in Massachusetts, yet he found the attraction of William Penn's experiment irresistible, and in 1693 he and his family relocated to Philadelphia. Having made this move, Shippen was immediately accepted as an influential member of the Quaker elite in Philadelphia and installed in a succession of important offices: in 1695, as a member of the assembly and its speaker; in 1696, as a member of the provincial council; in 1697, as a justice of the provincial supreme court; in 1701, as mayor of Philadelphia. His third marriage, however, occurring in 1706, did not conform with Quaker practice, and the all too evident confirmation of intimacy with his bride preceding their marriage caused scandal among his coreligionists. In subsequent generations, the Shippens abandoned the Society of Friends and joined the Willings as members of the Anglican community.[27]

Charles Willing and Ann Shippen were married in Christ Church on January 21, 1731. They would have a large family of eleven children, only one of whom died in infancy. On the birth of his third son in 1744, Charles Willing rejoiced in a letter to his friend: "Mrs. Charles Willing has lately brot me another Fine Boy; and I still flatter myself by my Endeavours Fortune will be as propitious to me in an Increase in Fortune, as it has been in mouths."[28] Fortune did indeed turn out to be doubly kind to him as his mercantile business and the wealth he realized from it expanded along with the size of his family. Like Edward Shippen before him, he rotated through an array of city offices, culminating in his election as mayor in 1748. While serving as mayor he began plans to build a comfortable townhouse on the southwest corner of Third Street and what soon would be called Willings Alley, that narrow east-west passageway linking Third and Fourth Streets. It was the first residence built in the open space on Third Street stretching southward to Spruce.[29]

On November 30, 1754, not much more than a year after the birth of his eleventh child, his daughter Margaret, Charles Willing died, succumbing to the rapid onset of a "nervous fever."[30] His eldest child, Thomas, had returned five years earlier from legal studies in London to join his father in trade under the firm name of Charles Willing and Son. As Thomas Willing recognized, it was on his shoulders that the responsibility would fall of caring for his siblings and his widowed mother and of maintaining the lucrative business his father had established. Among the more than two dozen letters he sent in December to correspondents of the firm announcing his father's death were two despairing letters to his uncle in England, whom he affectionately addressed "Dear Nunk." Pleading for counsel from this trusted source, he confided, "[E]very moment I am more and more sensible of my unhappy Situation & that of so large a Family. God knows what may become of them bereft of their Protector and Direction. My Fathers Affairs are widely scattered abroad, & it will require much time & assiduity to collect and settle them. If I have Life and health I may be able to do it." A particular embarrassment he mentioned to his uncle was that his father had neglected to change his will as more children were born, producing a painful imbalance in legacies.[31]

Another matter weighed on Thomas Willing's mind. His sister Dorothy remained at home under a cloud. The year before their father died she had eloped with a British naval officer, probably a friend of Thomas Willing's, and was married in an irregular ceremony of which her parents had no warning.

Family legend had it that when Charles Willing heard the news, he collapsed, striking the back of his head a severe blow, from which he never fully recovered. Only in the closing days of his life was he reconciled with this errant couple, and then without the consolation of knowing that his new, painfully acquired son-in-law would later become Captain Sir Walter Stirling, knighted for his services to the Crown. As surrogate for his deceased father, Thomas Willing had to reckon with the challenge of five unmarried sisters, ranging in age from less than two to twenty-two. Though but ten at the time, Elizabeth Willing could hardly have forgotten the drama caused when her sister Dolly ran off with Walter Stirling.[32]

Elizabeth Willing was the sixth of eleven children born to Charles and Ann Willing. When she was christened at Christ Church on September 15, 1743, her age was entered in the church records as seven months, five days, or a birth date that would be translated to February 21 under the reformed Gregorian calendar that the English-speaking world belatedly adopted in 1752.[33] Of her own childhood practically nothing is known. Many years later, in a letter of condolence to her niece following her sister Mary Byrd's death, she recalled a part of the past she had shared with her sister: "our youth was passed in a reciprocity of kind conciliatory offices, and unbounded confidence, for at least fifteen years we [she and her sister Mary] occupied the same Chamber."[34] Half of the period when the two sisters roomed together was spent in the spacious but crowded house on the corner of Third Street and Willings Alley, the construction of which was completed after their father's death. As illustration of the "unbounded confidence" she referred to, the Powel House today owns a charming miniature of the young Elizabeth Willing, painted at about the time her sister married William Byrd III, of Westover, Virginia, in 1761. In this first portrayal of Elizabeth Willing, she is shown wearing a double-strand pearl choker and a low-cut red dress, trimmed with lace and sporting a large blue bow (see front cover). Prim and composed, she appears wholly immune to any concern about a future yet to unfold for her.[35]

As both the eldest child and first son, Thomas Willing went to England at an early age to receive a privileged upper-class education that culminated in his studying for the bar at the Inner Temple.[36] Although his sisters may not have attended any established school in Philadelphia, their education was far from neglected. The Willing family could have easily afforded private tutors for the girls, and judging from the many letters of theirs that remain, they benefited from superior instruction. They had a thorough command not just of spelling and grammar, which alone would have distinguished them from many of their contemporaries of similar background, but also of style and expressiveness in their writing.[37] The credit for this training belonged to their mother who was from the outset a steadying influence in the Charles Willing household. In 1738, to set a proper example of religious observance, she approached the baptismal font at Christ Church and received as an adult, along with her infant child, the sacramental initiation that was omitted in the years of her own Quaker upbringing.[38] From a vantage point in midlife, her daughter Elizabeth testified to the crucial role a mother plays in the education of her children, and especially of her daughters:

> To Educate a Child in such a manner as to fit her for receiving & communicating Happiness is certainly the most arduous Task that can devolve on the female Character. Yet certain it is that the Groundwork of Education with both Sexes rests on the Mother. She gives the first & most lasting Impressions. Even the Language must be taught by her & is therefore properly denominated the Mother Tongue. Is it not then wonderfull that Men, in all Ages, shou'd be so totally regardless of female Education?

It may also have reflected the instruction this daughter of Ann Willing received that she excluded from the curriculum appropriate for young women subjects such as "the abstruse Sciences or dead Languages," which in her judgment "the natural vivacity of our Sex totally unfits us for."[39]

Thomas Willing remained a bachelor until he was thirty-two. After his marriage to Ann McCall in 1763, the family house on Third Street began to fill up rapidly with their children.[40] As the oldest sister in residence who had yet to marry, Elizabeth came under increasing pressure to do so as the decade wore on, whether that pressure was self-imposed or not. Rumor linked her name with the celebrated author of *Letters from a Farmer in Pennsylvania*, John Dickinson, ten years her senior, who would eventually move from the status of outspoken patriot to withholding his vote for independence, as her brother Thomas Willing also did.[41] In the summer of 1768, Elizabeth wrote to her sister Mary Byrd in Virginia that, notwithstanding the report of her forthcoming engagement, "universally talked of here," there was no truth to the story. If there were, "it would not be necessary for you to enquire of me . . . as my dear Colonel Byrd & yourself shou'd be among ye first I would communicate such a piece of intelligence to." Mary Byrd would have come to her own conclusion when her sister urged her to read the "Farmers Letter"—because of the strength of its argument and not "because I am supposed to be attached to ye amiable Author," whom Elizabeth insisted she would admire for his work even "if he was my greatest Enemy."[42]

Her immediate romantic inclinations put to the side, Elizabeth Willing betrays in this message what would be for her an enduring passion, an interest in issues of political moment and statecraft, a domain in her lifetime and for long afterwards that men believed exclusively theirs. She maintained that interest almost in spite of herself. As a married woman, she lectured this same sister on avoiding political engagements of any kind:

> [A] fine Woman is totally unfit for Government & what are commonly called the great Affairs of public Life. [Women] are quick at Expedient, ready in the Moment of sudden Exigencies, excellent to suggest, but their Imagination runs Riot; it requires the vigor of Mind alone possessed by Men to digest & put in Force a Plan of any Magnitude. There is a natural precipitancy in our Sex that frequently frustrates its own Designs.[43]

On August 7, 1769, the Reverend Jacob Duché officiated at a wedding ceremony in Christ Church uniting Elizabeth Willing and Samuel Powel in marriage.[44] If not his wife's first choice, Samuel Powel had wealth, education, and solid credentials in the Philadelphia establishment, which recommended him as a suitor. His grandfather, Samuel Powell, known as the "rich carpenter," was among the first arrivals in the province of Pennsylvania. He had prospered from the combination of his trade as a carpenter, his investments in real estate, and a marriage of strategic value in the Quaker community. His father, another Samuel Powel (who abbreviated the family name by dropping the second "l"), having succeeded as a merchant, died nine years before the first Samuel did. Upon his grandfather's death in 1756, the third Samuel therefore came into a large fortune, the result, as Deborah Logan bluntly put it, of his ancestors' working "at the muck-rake to some purpose." After his graduation from the nascent College of Philadelphia in 1759, this Samuel Powel followed the example of other young men of his background and means by going abroad to increase his knowledge of the world. What in the typical case might have been a year's absence, or two at the most, lasted seven years, until he was forced to return home to look after the substantial property he had inherited.[45]

By that time the attractions of Britain and the Continent had exerted a powerful hold on the rich carpenter's grandson. He traveled extensively, hobnobbing with the very best of enlightened Europe wherever he went. In 1764 he and his good friend from Philadelphia, John Morgan, a physician then in serious postgraduate training, made their way to Rome to take in all the sights, to enroll in art courses, to have their portraits painted by the beguiling Angelica Kauffmann, and to be received in private audience by Pope Clement XIII. On the way back to England, they made a pilgrimage to the sage of Ferney, Voltaire, who, after a pleasant visit in which he exercised his English, dispatched them with this rallying cry, a variant of his "*Écrasez l'infâme!*": "Hate Hypocrisy, Hate Masses & above all Hate the Priests."[46]

During this extended period abroad, Samuel Powel shed whatever was left—and probably not much was—of his birthright Quaker heritage. He was baptized an Anglican, as John Morgan, also a former Quaker, had been before him. Upon Powel's return to Philadelphia, the Philadelphia Monthly Meeting appointed two Friends to confer with him and ascertain his religious commitment. They reported back to the meeting his emphatic statement that "he never looked upon himself as belonging to our Society . . . [and] that the Decision he had come into in joining with another Society, was not sudden, but from a result of Judgment, and desired that Friends might not concern themselves further about him." As this declaration appeared "very opposite to that Meekness and Self denial becoming the Religious Profession we make," the meeting instructed Israel Pemberton, in what seems a face-saving gesture, to inform Powel that he could no longer be considered "a Member of our Religious Society."[47]

Five days before he married Elizabeth Willing, Samuel Powel took title to a large house and generous land area a short distance south of the Willing mansion on Third Street. Three stories in height, topped by dormer space, with a west wing of two stories and a full basement, this structure began to take shape in 1765. Immediately adjoining to the north was the house of similar design that William and Mary Byrd had built shortly after their marriage. The first owner of what is now called the Powel House was Charles Stedman, a Scottish merchant who, faced with financial reverses, advertised the property for sale in 1766. Even though the house was largely completed in his ownership, Stedman may never have occupied it.[48] As far as the Powels were concerned, they would not feel comfortably at home until further work was done to achieve a standard of elegance consistent with their social status and Samuel Powel's wealth. Turning to Philadelphia's finest craftsmen to decorate the principal rooms of their new house, they concentrated their attention on the front room that ran the full width of the second floor. Very likely, it was Hercules Courtenay who carved the richly ornamented mantel and overmantel in that room, and James Clow who was responsible for the elaborate complementary design of its plaster ceiling. This front room and the slightly less lavishly ornamented withdrawing room to the rear exemplify the high rococo style so prized in Philadelphia interiors during the second half of the eighteenth century.[49]

From the time of his marriage forward, Samuel Powel gradually recedes into the background. No longer are his opinions and enthusiasms recorded in journal entries and personal correspondence of the kind he left to document his grand tour (or escape) of the 1760s. Instead, one takes measure of him in meticulous bookkeeping entries as he manages his wealth and writes polite and then pointed letters to tenants delinquent in the payment of their rent; in official positions to which he was appointed or elected; in board minutes of various organizations with which he was affiliated; and in the recurrent discharge of his responsibilities as a presumably amiable host. Did he have a deeper, more intellectual side for which we may fail to give him sufficient credit? Though clearly conceiving it as a compliment, Bishop William White ascribed a particular quality to Powel that he thought his friend possessed "in a very singular Degree." In recommending Powel for service as a charitable trustee, White wrote that "he is minutely attentive to whatever Business he undertakes."[50] A much later observer, looking at what is left of the record, might judge Powel a reformed bon vivant, someone who had traded nonchalance for punctiliousness (a progression exactly the opposite of what customarily occurred in the passage from Quakerism to Anglicanism). It is only on rare occasion that there emerges a more finely etched profile of him, as when, for example, he prepares with a draftsman's precision plans and specifications for a house to be built in Roxborough, or lists books he has purchased for his impressive library, or copies out a long excerpt in French from Lavater's work on physiognomy that intrigued him.[51]

With its decoration and furnishings, the house on Third Street was intended to impress guests received there. One such guest, John Adams, was duly impressed when, as a delegate to the First Continental Congress, he joined a numerous company at a party the Powels gave on September 8, 1774. In his diary and letters home to Abigail during this period, as the out-of-town delegates were treated to one sumptuous meal after another in the best houses of Philadelphia, his Puritan principles appear to have come under constant attack. Of the entertainment at the Powels, he bemoaned, "A most sinfull Feast again! Every Thing which could delight the Eye, or allure the Taste. . . . " Nor was that the end of it: after having consumed his portion of "Punch, Wine, Porter, Beer &tc. &tc.," he tested his remaining sobriety by climbing to the top of the Christ Church steeple, where he and a few others similarly motivated could admire the thriving city spread out before them.[52]

To permit such festive occasions, to ensure their own personal comfort and ease, and, not least of all, to keep up appearances in Philadelphia society, Samuel and Elizabeth Powel required an ample staff of servants. Those they first recruited would have included help for both inside and outside the house: a gardener, a coachman, more than one maid, and a cook of proven ability. If the names, characters, and specific duties of these servants are, for the most part, unknown, the detailed records that exist for the Chew family, occupying the adjoining house originally built for William Byrd and his wife that Benjamin Chew subsequently acquired, give a good idea of the staffing pattern and its depth for an admittedly much larger household than the Powels had.[53]

Like Benjamin Chew, Samuel Powel owned slaves. Less than a year after Jacob Duché had performed the same service for the Powels, the marriage register of Christ Church records that he united in marriage Samuel, "the

Negro slave of Mrs. Higgins," and Fanny, the slave of "Mr. Powel." Elsewhere one learns that in October 1773 Powel purchased from William Jenkins "a Negro Wench called Hagar" for the sum of one hundred pounds. In the provincial tax list for 1774, Samuel Powel's reportable assets included but one slave and one bound servant, at the uniformly established values of four pounds and one pound ten shillings, respectively. Either by manumission or by sale, Powel would dispose of the slaves he owned, so that by the first federal census of 1790, no one appeared in that category in the Powel household, although Benjamin Chew next door was recorded in that census as owning three slaves.[54]

For the Chews, the Powels, and others of their class, probably the servant most in demand was a competent cook. The critical role that this servant played in ensuring domestic harmony comes through in an icily civil letter that Elizabeth Powel felt compelled to send to Mrs. Alexander Wilcocks just after New Year's Day, 1781. Mrs. Wilcocks evidently complained that Mrs. Powel had lured away Betty Smith without giving her former employer the opportunity to provide herself "with another in so important a Station as that of a Cook." Betty Smith's new employer protested that "I should be much pained to think that the meanest Person could imagine me capable of so indelicate & ungenerous a Procedure." In defense of her conduct Elizabeth Powel went to great lengths to set forth the several interviews she had with Betty Smith, the precautions she took to obtain a satisfactory reference of her character from Mrs. Wilcocks, the concern she expressed that Betty give adequate notice, and the unhappiness this contested servant said she had experienced in her previous place of employment. In the end, Elizabeth Powel concluded that "there could be no Reason of Honor or Delicacy" to prevent her from taking on Betty Smith, who was, she pointed out, "a free woman," fully able to plot her own course.[55]

Though it may not have been quite the rosy picture Philadelphia's first historian, John Fanning Watson, painted in retrospect of "the old time" when slaves "felt themselves an integral part of the family to which they belonged" and "were a happier class of people than the free blacks of the present day [1830] generally are," it is a permissible inference that, from an early date, the Powels were especially solicitous about the welfare of their servants, whether slaves, indentured, or free. Samuel Powel in brief testamentary dispositions and his wife in much more elaborate ones provided generously for their servants. In the will she signed in 1795 after she became a widow, Elizabeth Powel called for continuing financial support to be given to William McLane, a young free black man, as "testimony of my gratitude" to McLane's grandfather, "our faithfull Coachman Joseph." In that same will she also gave lifetime annuities to two free black women who "formerly lived with us" and whom she described as "faithfull honest affectionate Servants."[56]

Husband and wife, the Powels envisioned their house on Third Street as being suitable for more than mere display and entertainment. They also hoped to raise children there.[57] In the Powel House today there is a poignant reminder of their shared objective: a child's wagon or go-cart, showing signs more of age than of wear and tear through hard use, on three of whose sides the painted monogram "SP" appears. Tradition has assigned the wagon, by dubious reckoning, to the childhood of Samuel Powel's father at the beginning of the eighteenth century; it would seem safer to conclude that Samuel Powel himself was the first user of the wagon and that he kept it for a son of his to enjoy, or alternatively that it was specially made for that much anticipated heir. On June 29, 1770, Elizabeth Powel gave birth to a son, who at baptism received his father's, grandfather's, and great-grandfather's name. This Samuel Powel died a year later and was buried in the Christ Church graveyard. A second son, born on June 26, 1775, also named Samuel, survived but two weeks before joining his brother in the same burial ground.[58]

It was by no means exceptional for parents at that time to lose children in infancy. Nevertheless, the Powels may have tried to take special precautions to bring their first-born child into the world safely. Samuel Powel's receipt book shows payment of the not inconsiderable sum of twenty-four pounds to William Shippen & Son in 1773 "for Medicines Supplied & Attendance on his family." If Elizabeth Powel experienced any apprehension during her pregnancy or after the delivery of her son in 1770, it would have been natural for her to consult her cousin, the younger William Shippen, who, following an apprenticeship with his father, obtained additional training in London and Edinburgh. William Shippen, Jr., became America's first specialist in obstetrical medicine and prenatal care; he not only advertised in the pages of the *Pennsylvania Gazette* that he had assisted a number of women through difficult pregnancies but he also offered a course of practical instruction for expectant mothers.[59]

In looking back some sixty years, Deborah Logan recalled "when a girl at school hearing the Bells of Christ Church ring a merry peal" upon the birth of Elizabeth Powel's son, "the only time I think I ever heard them upon such an occasion." She went on to record in her diary that this child did not survive infancy, "it died of the small pox for which it was innoculated [*sic*] by Dr. Morgan, a great friend of its fathers who was Patronised by him."[60] Morgan had become William Shippen, Jr.'s, archrival in the medical profession, the competition between them turning to outright hostility.[61] As a strong proponent of inoculation, and notwithstanding the professional presence of the Shippens, Morgan may have entered the scene as Samuel Powel's intimate friend to inoculate his infant son. There is no independent confirmation of Deborah Logan's recollection, except another, later entry in Samuel Powel's receipt book showing payment to John Morgan of eight pounds seven shillings "for Medicine & Attendance on his Family."[62]

Though death may have routinely claimed the lives of infant children in eighteenth-century Philadelphia, Elizabeth Powel's loss of her first-born child remained for her a grievous blow. She would keep close at hand a lock of her son's hair and these lines of poetic lament she penned on a sheet of black-bordered paper:

Beneath this Hillocks narrow bound
A lovely Infant lies,
Till the last Trumpet shakes the Ground
And rolls away the Skies.
From all the Chequer'd Ills below
Sammy secure shall sleep;
His little Heart no Pain shall know,
His Eyes no more shall weep.
Some pitying Angel view'd the Lamb,
In Innocence array'd
And snach'd him from each future Snare
The World and guile had laid.
When Thousands rising from the Dust
Shall tremble as they rise.
This smiling Saint, without Distrust
Shall upward lift his Eyes.[63]

The deaths of two sons bearing his name could not have left Samuel Powel unmoved. To help him cope with that loss, he may have sought the distraction provided by public service. In 1775, the year of his second son's birth and death, the Philadelphia Common Council elected Samuel Powel the city's mayor, the last to occupy that position before the Revolution. Guidebooks today often refer to him as Philadelphia's "Patriot Mayor," implying that he actively supported the Revolutionary cause, a commitment which, however, cannot be readily substantiated.[64]

His nearest neighbors on Third Street—James Wilson at the corner of Third and Walnut; his wife's brother Thomas Willing at the corner of Willings Alley; and Benjamin Chew, who had succeeded to the ownership of the Byrd house next door—were all suspected of loyalist sympathies.[65] Clearly not compelled to leave because he was then targeted as the "Patriot Mayor," Samuel Powel and his wife stayed in Philadelphia during the British occupation of the city from September 1777 to June 1778. He had, of course, the strongest incentive to remain in order to protect his substantial real estate holdings, including the house on Third Street with its valuable contents.

Only at the very end of the British occupation of the city was his house commandeered, and then for a period of less than two weeks in June 1778 when the Earl of Carlisle and his entourage moved in, requiring the Powels to retreat to the two-story west wing of the house reserved for their servants. The head of an ill-starred peace mission appointed by Lord North, the Earl of Carlisle landed in Philadelphia just as Sir William Howe's recently appointed replacement, General Henry Clinton, the forces he commanded, and those Americans who had collaborated with the enemy were packing up to leave.[66] Of his temporary displacement of the Powels, Carlisle wrote a friend:

> I am not, I own, quite at my ease; for coming into a gentleman's house, without asking his leave, taking possession of all of the best apartments, and placing a couple of sentrys at his door, using his plate, etc., etc, are very repugnant to my disposition. I make him and his wife a visit every day, talking politics with them, and we are the best friends in the world. They are very agreeable, sensible people, and you would never be out of their company.[67]

It would be unfair to read too much into this display of amiability toward an uninvited guest. Yet, after the many pleasant years he had spent in England and lacking any great investment in the outcome, either material or philosophical, Samuel Powel could have adjusted with relative equanimity to a result in the war quite different from the one that eventually occurred.

In the spring of 1778, Elizabeth Powel sent a letter to her sister Anne Francis that gives some notion of how the Powels were surviving the occupation. She explained her failure to reply to previous messages as arising from "a certain irksomeness when our Letters are liable to be read by every Impertinent." She sympathized with the trials that her sister and her husband were undergoing as they had taken refuge in Paradise, a property by that ironic name that they owned in New Jersey. They had given their newly born daughter the name Elizabeth with the avowed thought that, should anything happen to them, Elizabeth Powel would become her guardian. Protesting that she needed no such inducement to accept that responsibility, the aunt trusted that the child's reported resemblance to her did not include constitutional weaknesses like "spasms and pains in my Head," which she attributed in part to Mr. Powel's "Rage . . . for large Fires" but which he dismissed as her "bad Nerves."

Her husband was also more detached than she about the destruction of family properties out of town, including the one owned by the Francises where Elizabeth Powel had gone in vain to rescue some of the furniture: "The devastation was begun & I really turned from it with Grief." Among "the thousand distresses that America feels at this time," Elizabeth Powel deplored "the want of proper Schools for the Instruction of youth . . . especially when the Barbarities of War have almost made Mankind savage." Concerning the inquiry her sister requested she make for a lost friend, she commented that "she [the friend] cannot have wanted Necessaries if she had been in Phila all the Winter."[68]

When he came to Philadelphia in November 1780, the Marquis de Chastellux (then Chevalier de Chastellux), soldier and philosophe combined, saw the scars of war in houses destroyed or burned, "monuments the English have left behind them." Yet "these ruins" presented, as he saw it, "only a picture of temporary misfortune," as if a sudden storm had swept through a city otherwise left largely intact and prosperous. Chastellux's *Travels in North America*, the account of the three years he spent in America as the Revolution was coming to an end, is characterized by his sympathetic yet perceptive views of those whom he encountered. At one of the first dinner parties he attended in Philadelphia, he met Samuel Powel, "a man of considerable fortune, but without any part in the government, his attachment to the common cause having hitherto appeared rather equivocal."[69]

Of Elizabeth Powel, whom he met a day or so later, he was equally candid in his assessment, so much so that, out of admiration for her, he felt compelled to tone down what he had originally written. In the first privately published edition of his *Travels*, he provides this portrait of her at home in the house on Third Street, the accuracy of which there is not the slightest reason to doubt:

> [C]ontrary to American custom, she plays the leading role in the family—*la prima figura*, as the Italians say. She received me in a handsome house furnished in the English manner and, what pleased me most, adorned with fine prints and some very good copies of the best Italian paintings, for Mr. Powel has traveled in Europe and has been in Rome and Naples, where he acquired a taste for the fine arts. As for Mrs. Powel, she had not traveled, but she has wit and a good memory, speaks well and talks a great deal; she honored me with her friendship and found me very meritorious because I meritoriously listened to her.

In the two volumes of the *Travels* published in France in 1786, Chastellux edited out the references to Mrs. Powel's loquaciousness and praised her instead for "what chiefly distinguishes her," which he more tactfully described as "her taste for conversation and the truly European manner in which she used her wit and knowledge."[70]

Whether she was able to trace its evolution or not, this compliment in its final version would have pleased Elizabeth Powel. In her circle of friends, in the frequent entertaining she and her husband did, in the correspondence of hers she was at pains to preserve, she cultivated a style of sophistication and politesse that in the Paris salon had been elevated to a high art form.[71] An alternative model, perhaps somewhat more accessible to her, would have been the bluestockings, the slightly derisive name used to identify those women of conversational talent and moral and intellectual vigor who held sway in London literary society during the second half of the eighteenth century.[72] Whichever model she followed (if she consciously followed either), she read widely, taking pride in the range of her interests and the independence of her judgment. Like a true salonnière, but not a bluestocking, she engaged, at least at this period in her life, in flirtatious behavior that one would run the risk of dismissing too quickly as altogether harmless. Yet, in the end, it is Chastellux's portrayal, emphasizing her American, less reserved side, that rings true. She spoke and wrote her mind freely, surrendering discretion to candor when she thought it appropriate to do so. It was a duty that affection repeatedly imposed on her, as letters she labored over illustrate.

Mary Byrd was tragically widowed when her distraught husband, weighed down by the burden of his debts and by the charge of loyalist sympathies, committed suicide on New Year's Day in 1777.[73] In consulting her younger sister about books that would be suitable reading for her children, Mary made the mistake of suggesting that Lord Chesterfield's *Letters to his Son* might provide useful instruction and, in doing so, evoked a long lecture from Philadelphia. Elizabeth Powel thought that Addison's contributions to *The Tatler* and the late eighteenth century's vade mecum of moral authority, *The Economy of Human Life,* were far preferable to Chesterfield. In spite of his "epistolary stile . . . perfectly adapted to the Design of his Work," his lordship showed a deplorable lack of sensitivity concerning the female sex: " . . . he mistook Appetite for Love & regarded the Object of his Inclination only as it could contribute to the gratification of his vicious desires." Then proceeding on a tangent that had little to do with a recommended reading list for her sister's children, Elizabeth dwelt on the danger for a married woman in taking pity on a man who tried to seduce her: too often "it places her on the verge of a Precipice," leading to "a total Transfer to her utter and inevitable Disadvantage."[74] Had she herself, we are left to wonder, teetered on the edge of that precipice?

Both in this letter and in one she sent the following year to Mary Byrd's daughter on the occasion of the latter's marriage, Elizabeth Powel warmed to a favorite subject: how women might receive their due in a male-dominated society. She promised her niece the Irish edition of Oliver Goldsmith's *History of the Roman Empire* as reading that "might be acceptable to you." Of perhaps more immediate value to the new bride, she also gave guidance on how "a Woman can hope to preserve her Empire with a Man of Sense & Sensibility." It requires, she wrote, "many sacrifices . . . [and] the nicest Delicacy of Conversation even in the most private Hours." The greatest sacrifice was required of a wife of "personal Accomplishments & a Mind well cultivated by a liberal Female Education," because "Men destined by Opinion & uncontrolled Custom, for the severer Studies which are to fit them for the public walk of Life . . . do not Love to find a Competitor in the softer Sex." To what extent, we are again obliged to ask, did her own experience—this time as a dutiful wife—inform the advice she gratuitously provided her niece?[75]

In this same period, Elizabeth Powel entrusted to her sister Margaret Hare, who was about to leave for Europe, a message to the Reverend Jacob Duché, the minister who had officiated at her wedding in Christ Church and who had lived in a comfortable house a few blocks away from the Powels on Third Street. At his death in 1798, Duché would leave behind a record of political and religious vacillation that bewildered his family and friends, for it was his habit constantly to repent his most recent conversion. Having delivered fervent patriotic prayers and sermons in the presence of members of the Continental Congress as the Revolution approached and having served briefly as Congress's chaplain after independence was declared, Duché turned loyalist when the British occupied Philadelphia in 1777. He addressed a bizarre and highly injudicious letter to George Washington in October of that year in which he attempted to explain his change of heart. He specifically named the "dregs of Congress" who were unworthy of Washington's leadership and personal sacrifice, while he also dismissed the hope of support from France as wholly illusory. By the end of 1777 he had retreated to England, a disgruntled expatriate.[76]

Beginning in 1783, with another letter addressed to Washington, Duché sought a rehabilitation that would permit him to return unscathed to his home country.[77] It was at that point that his old friend and neighbor felt she had to intervene: "Think not of it my amiable Friend," she wrote in a letter she gave Margaret Hare to deliver in person as her sister embarked on a trip abroad, "exert your good Sense & Philosophy & endeavor to be happy in your present Exile." She recalled "the thousand Hours we have passed at our fire Side with you, in innocent and instructive Conversation" as evidence of the attachment she and her husband had to Duché. The error that in her judgment counted most heavily against him was his having claimed on the title page of his sermons published in London that he remained the rector of Christ Church and St. Peter's in Philadelphia. Though she supposed his "worthy Successor," the Reverend William White, later to be consecrated in London the first bishop of the Episcopal diocese of Pennsylvania, "would be happy to see you restored to every Thing that could contribute to your Felicity," Duché's titular presumption had "roused such a Spirit of Resentment against you with Persons that you must unavoidably mix with" that she could not conceive of a tolerable basis for his return. In the event, Duché was forced to postpone his homecoming until 1792 when Pennsylvania repealed its laws against Tories. Although there is no indication that, upon his return, the Powels welcomed him with open arms, neither did his old friend shun him completely. At his death in early 1798, Elizabeth Powel wrote Martha Washington: "My much valued friend the Rev. Mr. Jacob Duché has taken his departure for the Regions of eternal bliss."[78]

In about 1782, she acquired another valued friend who was much younger than she and more judicious than Jacob Duché. Encouraged by a famous uncle who gave his personal note to cover the hefty tuition fee, Bushrod Washington began law studies in Philadelphia by working in an apprentice capacity with James Wilson. His distinguished career in the law would culminate in long service on the United States Supreme Court as the successor to the man who trained him.[79] While he pursued his studies with Wilson, he became Elizabeth Powel's protégé. The affectionate relationship that developed between them would continue until his death a few months before hers; in her will she had provided for "Judge Washington [to receive] twenty Guineas to purchase a piece of plate as an evidence of my friendship and respect for his Virtues."[80]

After leaving Philadelphia in 1785, Bushrod Washington sent a number of letters to Elizabeth Powel that went unanswered for a time. She teasingly prefaced her delayed reply by saying that she had to pause before breaking "an established Rule of never writing to a Gentleman that does not correspond with Mr. Powel." What, she inquired, did Washington think of the book she had given him on revealed religion? Its author, in her opinion, had effectively countered "Hume and all the deistical writers," whose reasoning was like that of "a professional Friend that would knock down the House without providing even a temporary Shelter & argue in Defence . . . that it had not a solid foundation." She moved on to Washington's diet and his excessive conviviality that were matters of concern to her: "Dancing till two or three o'clock in the Morning, confined Air, the Vapor from a number of Candles, & still greater Breaths, are not beneficial to any one but I think peculiarly unfavorable to your Constitution." As for her own health, she confided that she had "such a severe attack of a cramp in my Breast" that she could not keep "off the Bed." That particular complaint had afflicted her for three years past and would not yield in the discomfort she experienced "even to Laudanum," without whose properties, however, as a "heavenly Medicine" she thought the globe would not be habitable.[81]

Elizabeth Powel repeatedly violated a cautionary precept of salonnières and bluestockings alike—by failing to avoid politics as a subject incompatible with refined conversation. She was incapable of withholding her opinion on the direction in which she saw her country moving, or on the competence of the leading figures in public life. Is it stretching things too much to suppose that she inherited some of this tendency from General Thomas Harrison, her great-great-grandfather, the regicide who went unrepentant to the gallows for his political beliefs?

Her sisters had the opportunity to reflect on this distinctive aspect of her character. Anne Francis in Philadelphia shared her concern with Mary Byrd in Virginia: "when in society she will animate and give a brilliancy to the whole Conversation, you know the uncommon command she has of Language and her ideas flow with rapidity. . . . I sometimes think her Patriotism causes too much Anxiety. Female politicians are always ridiculed by the other Sex."[82]

In the spate of biographies published to celebrate the tercentenary of Benjamin Franklin's birth, an old story has resurfaced, of an exchange between Franklin and Elizabeth Powel at the time the Constitutional Convention was winding up its business in Philadelphia in September 1787. The story, an attractive set piece, is designed to allow a venerable sage to perform at his epigrammatic best. In its early telling, it may be traced to James McHenry, the Secretary of War in George Washington's second administration. One of Franklin's recent biographers begins by describing "an anxious lady by the name of Mrs. Powel," which, in its vision of an obscure woman, something of a busybody beset by nervousness, is not an introduction that Elizabeth Powel would have cherished. According to the story, she approached Benjamin Franklin as he was leaving the State House to query him on what form of government the delegates had at last agreed to: "A republic, madam, if you can keep it," Franklin is said to have answered.[83]

After this tale had achieved currency in the quarter century following the convention's work, the anxious lady in question was called upon to verify it. Elizabeth Powel admitted embarrassment in denying "a conversation supposed to have passed between Dr. Franklin and myself respecting the goodness, and probable permanence of the constitution of these United States." A similar version of the tale had been published to her knowledge "in Poulson's Paper, I forget of what date," while another she traced to "the late secretary of War." Though she had no memory of accosting Franklin in this manner or of his memorable rejoinder, if indeed he delivered it, she retained a clear recollection of having "associated with the most respectable, influential Members of the Convention that framed the Constitution, and that the all important Subject was frequently discussed at our House." If so, a hostess always intrigued by political matters may have been complicit in a breach of the rule of strict secrecy that bound the delegates in their deliberations. And if such indiscreet disclosures had occurred in her drawing room, what need would there have been to descend in the public street on "the justly venerated patriotic, philanthropist Dr. Franklin" for information already obtained at home? [84]

Elizabeth Powel's most daring foray into politics concerned George Washington. The candor and familiarity she employed in advising this intimidating personality simply take one's breath away. The Powels had formed a close friendship with George and Martha Washington that went back to the time Washington served as a delegate to the First Continental Congress and made the rounds in September and October of 1774 as a dinner guest of many prominent Philadelphians.[85] In taciturnity and reserve and in a shared enthusiasm for agricultural pursuits, George Washington and Samuel Powel were a matched pair. In contrast, though they were on very good terms, Martha

Washington lacked much of Elizabeth Powel's sophistication and her flair for writing.[86] Over the years the two couples exchanged gifts and hospitality, as, for example, when the Powels visited the Washingtons at Mount Vernon in the autumn of 1787 after the Constitutional Convention had concluded its business in Philadelphia. During the many times Washington was in Philadelphia as soldier and statesman, he was a frequent visitor to the house on Third Street. He went there, of course, as an honored guest at many large parties the Powels gave, but more often than not, one has to think, simply for tea and sympathy. Without suggesting anything improper, the great drawing power was Elizabeth Powel, a woman of spirit and intelligence in whom he could safely confide.[87]

And confide in her he did, in a meeting they had at the presidential mansion one Thursday in November of 1792. He told her that he was seriously considering retiring from the presidency at the end of his first term, then fast approaching. Two days later she sat down and composed a seven-page letter that might have seemed to its recipient, in tone and content, as provocative as the letter Jacob Duché had sent in 1777. Both Duché and Elizabeth Powel began with protests of friendship and great admiration before presuming to tell Washington where his sense of duty should summon him. But, in contrast to Duché, who advocated surrendering to superior British forces, Elizabeth Powel urged Washington to hold fast in the face of enemy opposition. "Your resignation," she wrote,

> wou'd elate the Enemies of good Government. . . . They would say that you were actuated by Principles of self-Love alone—that you saw the Post was not tenable with any Prospect of adding to your Fame. The antifederalist would use it as an argument for dissolving the Union, and would urge that you, from Experience, had found the present System a bad one, and had, artfully, withdrawn from it that you might not be crushed under it Ruins. . . .

If she were to concede the point on which Washington undoubtedly insisted in their interview, "that there are Abilities and Virtues in other Characters Equall to the Task," she nevertheless found "confidence in those Abilities and that Integrity" critically lacking. She then proceeded to marshal her arguments. She asserted that "at this time, you are the only Man in America that dares to do right on all public Occasions." She praised his self-control, or as she put it, the "Empire over yourself," while pleading that he not "yield that Empire" to "a Love of Ease . . . or a false Diffidence of Abilities." And in her last, perhaps boldest thrust, she appealed to Washington's sense of self-esteem: "That you are not indifferent to the Plaudits of the world I must conclude when I believe that the love of honest Fame has and ever will be predominant in the best, the noblest and the most capable Natures. Nor is the approbation of Mankind to be disregarded with Impunity even by you."[88]

George Washington never replied in writing to this extraordinary message, which he preserved in his papers. Yet he does not appear to have taken offense at the lecture he received on where duty called him. In fact, he may have regarded the close reasoning in his confidante's long letter as all but irrefutable. Whatever reaction he had, the relationship between the Washingtons and the Powels continued to be a warm one as the two couples entered a new year.

4

Deciphering the Portrait's Message

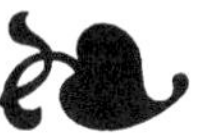

THE YEAR 1793 BEGAN AUSPICIOUSLY in Philadelphia. It would end in deep tragedy.

When the votes of the electors were tallied in early February, George Washington was unanimously reelected president. That result had become a foregone conclusion once he allowed his silence on the issue of a second term to speak for itself. He came to that decision, he told Thomas Jefferson, after receiving "strong solicitations" in Philadelphia.[89]

The conjunction of Elizabeth Powel's fiftieth birthday on February 21, the president's sixty-first a day later, and the second inauguration on March 4 produced sustained celebrating in Philadelphia. In the ritual observance of his own birthday on February 22, the president accepted the tendered best wishes of both the House of Representatives and the Senate. However, he felt that because of the recent death of a nephew, it would have appeared improper for his wife and him to join in the conspicuous gaiety at the house on Third Street the night before. He sent a message of regret offering "the compliments of the day to Mrs. Powel" and expressing the hope that with "the return of many anniversaries . . . her happiness may increase."[90]

Elizabeth Powel's fiftieth birthday party must have been what we, in our colloquial idiom, would call "a blast." Among those who attended, it certainly left a lasting impression. In late January 1830, two weeks after Elizabeth Powel had died, Samuel Breck paid tribute in his diary to "a sensible woman," as he recalled "thirty-seven years ago [when] I was one of a large party in her house to celebrate her fiftieth birthday. It was a ball numerously attended, given in February 1793."[91] Drawing on the report of a family member who had been there, a great-nephew who was born more than a decade after the event wrote that the ball had "a good deal of éclat. It was opened by herself in a Minuet, with Barbé-Marbois, the French Minister, both dressed . . . in blue satin trimmed with squirrel skins, to match."[92] Toasts were proposed in dizzying succession. A neighbor, the widower Henry Hill, had prepared a poem of questionable taste to recite for the occasion:

Proceed Eliza—Forty-nine
Can charm, persuade, enchant, and shine;
Yet, when you sweetly tell me true
"Sixteen for sixty ne'er will do,"
Alas! It chills me thr'o and thr'o.
Desire and reason are at Strife,
And fight about a Dreg of Life.

But, oh! When a fair Breast I view
Of matchless Mould and tempting Hue
Or gaze, entranced, on radiant eyes,
Desire prevails, Reflection dies.

Like driven Snow I melt away
Expos'd to Sol's meridian ray.
Old Sixty, then, is not the Truth
I'm Twenty One, a vigorous Youth.[93]

In retrospect, Eliza's reaching fifty in 1793 might have seemed the perfect time to have her portrait painted, albeit by an artist of greater refinement than Henry Hill. Matthew Pratt was not, however, commissioned to portray a joyous subject or a celebratory occasion.

A mild winter gave way to a halcyon spring and to a summer that was torrid even by Philadelphia standards. By early August it became apparent that a fatal pestilence had invaded the city. Officials of the federal and state governments, merchants like Henry Drinker whose townhouse was in the heart of the infected district, professionals not bound in conscience to minister to the sick—in short, all who could leave the city—deserted en masse and took refuge in more sheltered country locations.[94] George and Martha Washington remained in the capital longer than it was wise to do so. As they prepared to move southward to Mount Vernon, they tried to persuade the Powels to accompany them. Elizabeth Powel explained why she could not bring herself to accept their invitation as long as her husband, then the speaker of the Pennsylvania Senate, insisted on staying: "The Possibility of his being ill during my Absence & thereby deprived of the Consolation and Aid he might derive from my Attention to him would be to me a lasting Source of Affliction."[95]

As it turned out, that is exactly what happened. Samuel Powel ignored the advice of Benjamin Rush to avoid the center of the city and in a trip to town contracted yellow fever. He died in the farmhouse located on his sprawling estate of Powelton on the west side of the Schuylkill, attended only by a loyal servant and a young doctor who hesitated to bleed his patient in the relentless manner prescribed by Rush. His wife was not present during his final hours. She had fled to her brother Richard's farm in Haverford Township, Delaware County. Her failure to be with Samuel Powel when he died became for her "a lasting Source of Affliction," as well as the cause for prolonged reflection on the vicissitudes of life.[96]

In his will, Samuel Powel made more than nominal gifts to his sister and his two nephews. He also gave one hundred pounds each to his servant Philip Roedel and to "Samuel Powel Perkins, an orphan, whom I have apprenticed to William Griffiths, House Carpenter, . . . to be paid to him when he shall attain the age of Twenty one years." All else he left to "my very dear and loving wife," whom he appointed as sole executrix of his will. As a result, Elizabeth Powel came into great wealth upon her husband's death, much of it represented by his extensive real estate holdings. Toward the end of 1795 she made her own will; because of the many people she wished to remember and the specific bequests she had in mind, it was a longer and more elaborate document than her husband's.[97] In neither this will nor the much later one that would take effect upon her death in 1830 did she refer to the portrait Pratt had painted of her in the revealing yellow dress and the destination she intended for it. Nevertheless, her two wills and Samuel Powel's will of 1788 must be examined in an attempt to decipher the Pratt portrait and to locate it in time.

Though Elizabeth Powel had safely survived the epidemic of 1793, she could not forget the awful visitation of that year and the continuing threat of its return. The house on Third Street was no longer a safe refuge. Her servants were as anxious and unsettled as she was. At the end of that fateful year, she inquired of Robert Morris whether an indentured servant lad of his, Jacob by name, might be available to shore up her beleaguered staff. In a courteous reply, Morris agreed, but with some reluctance, to assign the indenture under which Jacob was bound for three more years of service for the sum of twenty pounds: "I have no desire that this Boy should be admitted into the service of Mrs. Powell [*sic*], neither will I object to it, altho I did intend to sell his time to some person who would provide hard Work for him as the proper reward for his Insolence."[98]

Elizabeth Powel's anguished state of mind was evident when she signed her will in 1795 and in a separate sealed letter of instructions for her youngest sister, Margaret Hare, to be opened only after receiving the news of her death. The first concern she expressed in that letter was about her servants: that they would be permitted to live in "my dwelling House at my Expense for Three Months after my Decease"; that their wages be continued for that period; and that "they may each have given to them a compleat Suit of Mourning."

What worried her even more, however, was the confirmation of her death and the arrangements for her funeral. As for many of her contemporaries, and not without some basis in experience, she shared a horror of premature burial. "It is my serious solemn INJUNCTION—that my body after being kept as long as it can with safety to Others be put into a red cedar Coffin . . . and that the cover or Lid not be put on or screwed down untill within a few Minutes of Interment." She desired to be buried in "the same Grave with my blessed departed Husband and Children" unless there be "any reasonable Objection" to her being buried in the city (presumably from a recurrence of yellow fever), in which case she stipulated that she be buried in the garden at Powelton, "in front of the House where my true tender constant Friend closed his excellent Life." She signed these sobering instructions "your affectionate afflicted widowed Sister, Eliza Powel."[99]

How long did this afflicted widow observe the conventions of strict mourning for her husband? On the eve of the eighth anniversary of his death, she declined, in the third person, the "affectionate invitation" of Mr. and Mrs.

Benjamin Chew, Jr., "in conformity with feelings (perhaps not quite under the control of Reason) and her Usage at this Period for the last Eight melancholy Years of her life."[100] However long that period of mourning was, Elizabeth Powel did not withdraw entirely from society or neglect the business at hand during it. Within a few months of Samuel Powel's death, she had taken charge of his books, estimated the income and expenses for the year ahead from his estate, and resumed his collection efforts by sending demand letters of escalating urgency that she copied from the samples he had left.[101]

She continued to receive family and friends in the house on Third Street. Her many relatives gathered there for Christmas dinner in 1797.[102] Nor did considerations of propriety make a widow of mature years any less inclined to engage in flirtatious behavior. Among the letters she received toward the end of the century, most were of a business nature, but one that she chose to keep was from a gentleman still reeling from his encounter with her the night before. "I had long done violence to my feelings," he began, "in not expressing what were their disposition towards you . . . but the Muse Madam has conquered prudence at last." Protesting that "my heart was really taken by surprize," he asked her to accept as sincere the "effusion of those sentiments" he had apparently poured forth the prior evening, as he signed himself "your affectionate."[103]

In regard to mourning dress, Elizabeth Powel would advise a bereaved friend many years later that she thought it primarily a matter of personal choice and convenience: "although it is generally worn it is by no means a sure symbol of either respect or affection."[104] Still, having so often identified herself in correspondence as the grieving widow and conscious as she always was of appearances, it is inconceivable that she would have worn in a portrait supposedly commemorating that grief the dress in which Pratt painted her. One gossipy reporter in Philadelphia at the end of the century wrote to her aunt that Elizabeth Powel remained in relative seclusion until George Washington's last birthday celebration as president in February 1797: "Mrs. Powel never goes into public though she sees both abroad and at home a good deal of company but on the Ball given to the President, as it was to be the last, she made her appearance at it. Drest in black velvet—I am told she look'd very well."[105]

Moreover, wholly apart from mourning etiquette, the bluestocking in her would have resisted the design of the dress in the portrait as constituting immodest exposure. Soon after Hannah More's novel *Coelebs in Search of a Wife* was published in 1808, Elizabeth Powel copied a passage from it to send to a friend as advice "every modest Female" should follow. Hannah More, a writer philanthropist, was a leading member of the bluestocking brigade. *Coelebs*, the only novel published among her various edifying works, enjoyed instant success. In characteristic fashion, Elizabeth Powel judged it a "very superior, but unequal Work." If women only knew, Hannah More expostulated in the passage Elizabeth Powel had singled out, "what was their real interest! If they could guess with what charms even the appearance of modesty invests the possessor, they would dress decorously from mere self love, if not from principle. The designing would assume modesty as artifice, the coquette would adopt it as an allurement . . . , and the voluptuous as the most infallible art of seduction."[106]

Piety of this kind had no appeal to Sydney Smith, an English clergyman who was also an assiduous letter-writer, but working in a lighter vein than Elizabeth Powel did. He had great fun at Hannah More's expense when, in a critical review of *Coelebs,* he pounced on the author's praise of modest dress: "If there is any truth to this passage, nudity becomes a virtue, and no decent woman in the future can be seen in garments."[107] Because she took very seriously her role as a source of uplifting advice, Mrs. Powel would not have been amused by this example of Sydney Smith's trenchant wit.

On the other hand, to portray Elizabeth Powel as a prude would be to misrepresent her. Reflecting on collars as a species of stays, she had a different lecture to deliver in November 1787 when her own youth was not so distant a memory. Good posture, she proclaimed, was as essential to health as to beauty, and young women should be taught to hold their heads up and throw their shoulders back. "It expands the Chest & prevents those ridiculous Distortions of the Face & Eyes which girls, at a certain age, frequently fall into from a foolish Bashfulness, or so the French call it a mauvaise haute. There are collars with Backs for the Shoulders; but this is so like putting them in Harness that I reprobate them, as I do all Ligatures on the human Form."[108]

The portrait Matthew Pratt painted shows Elizabeth Powel, unbound, not in mourning for her husband who died in 1793, but rather for her "beloved offspring," her two sons who died twenty years before. The key word is found on the funerary urn to her left in her portrait. That word is "Pledg[e]" (or perhaps its plural). In a figurative usage now bordering on the archaic, the *Oxford English Dictionary* gives this definition of "pledge" as a noun: "Applied to a child, as a token or evidence of mutual love and duty between parents, or as a hostage given to fortune." Then, by way of an especially touching illustration in relation to the portrait and its veiled meaning, the *OED* quotes this fragment from the verse of a seventeenth-century poet laureate: "No male Pledge, to give a lasting name, Sprung from his bed." Elizabeth Powel had frequent recourse to the pledge metaphor as, for example, when she wrote in 1814 about the "dear helpless pledges" of her great-niece's union or when she presented a gift of silver plate a year later to her nephew with the request that on his death "your Son one of the dear Pledges of your happy union may possess this Trifle." Most significant of all, in a long memorandum of wounded regret that she composed for her own purposes in 1813, she used these very words to describe the sons she had lost in infancy as "the dear pledges of a happy union."[109]

Yet if the portrait cannot reasonably be dated as late as 1793, when and under what circumstances did Matthew Pratt paint it? At the outset one must admit there is no absolutely clear answer to this question: no letter of Elizabeth Powel's to a relative or friend confirming the commission, no written instructions to Pratt concerning the sitter's idiosyncratic wishes, no ledger book entry or receipt showing payment to Pratt for the completed work.[110] The mystery that surrounds the painting is compounded because, over a period of several generations stretching well into the nineteenth century, no mention of the portrait appears in the extensive Powel family papers. So unyielding is the record that one has to question whether the portrait ever hung in any house Elizabeth Powel occupied before the Pennsylvania Academy of the Fine Arts delivered it on loan to the Powel House in 2000. Therefore, to come to any understanding of the portrait and the message behind it requires venturing onto uncertain ground and speculating about, among other things, a source of particular tension that may have affected Samuel and Elizabeth Powel's marital relationship.

Samuel Powel signed his will on June 20, 1788. He left his personal property outright to his wife, but to the gift he made to her of his large holdings in real estate he attached a significant condition, which was that "my wife not [be] pregnant at the time of my decease." If she were, one half of his real estate was to be held in trust until the after-born child reached the age of twenty-one, whereupon that child would acquire full ownership of the share. It would have made more sense in the interpretation of his will if he had provided for an equal division among his children who survived him, including any subsequently born child, for, in a strict reading of the language he used, he risked excluding as a beneficiary a child who might have been born during his lifetime. Did a sudden illness cause him to sign a hastily prepared will and to enlist as witnesses his pastor, Bishop William White, and Dr. John Jones, who would later attend Benjamin Franklin in his last illness? Samuel Powel's participation two weeks later, as president of the Philadelphia Society for Promoting Agriculture, in the grand federal procession celebrating both the Declaration of Independence and the newly ratified Constitution would appear inconsistent with any strong signal he might have received concerning his impending death. A more plausible explanation is that, in resorting to this awkward language, he betrayed the remote hope he still clung to that his wife might give birth to a child who would continue the Powel family line.[111]

For her part Elizabeth Powel had sadly laid aside any such possibility. In the summer of 1786, she allowed to a Virginia acquaintance of hers that "I have passed my Fortieth Year" (which was but a slight elision of her actual age). What she had come to regret, she wrote, was a wasted opportunity shared with others of her sex: "I have often thought that had we devoted ourselves with half the Ardor to the culture of our Minds that we too generally allot to our Persons, we should find more gratefull Returns & be certain of reaping a plentifull Harvest in the barren Season of old Age." At that very time and well before her husband had made the final dispositions in his will, she had turned her attention to her sister Margaret's son who was born in April of 1786.[112]

Sensitive to the feelings of the childless couple, Margaret Hare and her husband decided that their son should be known as John Powel Hare. To this nephew his aunt would soon transfer all of her pent-up maternal affection. As an infant he was sent to the Powels to escape scarlet fever. When in spite of this precaution he contracted it, his aunt nursed him back to health and later told him that he became "dear to her from my sufferings." Reaching school age, he spent every weekend as a routine matter with his aunt and uncle. Whether Samuel Powel was as attached as his wife was to their nephew is less clear. Years afterward it would fit essentially in the nephew's view of the past to represent that his wealthy uncle had until his death shown "great affection and solicitude for me" and that "[h]e gratified me in every shape, as a father."[113]

When her nephew came of age and left on a grand tour, not unlike the one on which his uncle Samuel Powel had gone in his youth, Elizabeth Powel assumed the entire cost of his trip and stay abroad. He carried with him a letter of introduction from Robert Hare, his father, to Richard Hare, his father's brother, who lived near London. Robert Hare struggled to explain in that letter the strange course events had taken. He recalled that Richard Hare had met the Powels during a prior visit to America when "they liv'd, in a handsome manner, in a large house, in Third Street, near Mrs. Willing's." Upon the birth of his youngest son, his sister-in-law, Robert Hart wrote, "appear'd to fix her eye upon him, as if to adopt him, for her own." As time passed she "uniformly appear'd, to retain the same predilection for him, which was signally manifested when he approach'd maturity" and she pressed him to take legal action to change his name to John Hare Powel. "For various reasons," as his father put it, "Mrs. Hare and I thought it proper to acquiesce in this proposal." Among the "various reasons" that may have influenced the Hares were the generous provisions Elizabeth Powel was prepared to make in her will for "my favorite nephew John Hare," on condition, however, that he assume the name of John Powel.[114]

Petitioned for that purpose in the year John Hare turned twenty-one, the Pennsylvania legislature passed an act that authorized the name change but that pointedly identified him as the son of Robert Hare. Though it has often been asserted that Elizabeth Powel adopted her nephew, there is no evidence that a formal legal adoption ever occurred. On the contrary, she consistently referred to him as her nephew in correspondence and in the wills she signed, while he, for his part, would emphatically insist that he remained the son of Robert and Margaret Hare. Because the first general adoption laws were not enacted in the United States until the middle of the nineteenth century, it would have necessitated special legislative action for Elizabeth Powel to displace her sister and brother-in-law as parents, a fundamental alteration in family ties that the statute changing his name clearly did not purport to accomplish.[115]

In the light of this fixation on her nephew, it seems closer to the mark to date the portrait circa 1786, or around the time when he was born and Elizabeth Powel despaired of becoming a mother again. To be sure, assigning an even earlier date to the portrait, nearer the dates of death of her own children, is an alternative that must be considered. In the limited genre of mourning portraits during the colonial period, of which Charles Willson Peale's *Rachel Weeping* is the most conspicuous example, it might seem that Pratt borrowed inspiration from the *Memorial to E. R.*, painted by his cousin James Claypoole, Jr. Claypoole signed and dated that portrait in Jamaica in 1774. More ambitious in thematic treatment than Pratt's, it depicts a young woman dressed in white with a lavender shawl over her shoulder who is accompanied by the allegorical figure of Fame. She points to a monument at her left on which rests a large funerary urn; verses appear inscribed on the monument's plinth; and, to top it off, two flying amorini are seen festooning the memorial piece with flowers (Figure 2). Yet, other than the fact that both artists were trained by the same craftsman, James Claypoole the elder, there is no reason to link these two paintings, in time or otherwise. Pratt probably never saw his cousin's work, because its provenance would suggest that it did not arrive in this country until a New Orleans antiquary acquired it from a London dealer in the twentieth century.[116]

Three considerations argue against dating the Pratt portrait of Elizabeth Powel much earlier than 1786: the apparent age of the person sitting for the portrait;[117] the lack of authenticated Pratt portraits during the Revolution, when of necessity he suspended his occupation; and the strong implication that the word "Farewe[ll]" on the funerary urn carries if uttered during the mid-1780s, for it is as if Elizabeth Powel were taking final leave of the children of her own conception in turning to a favored nephew to act as their proxy. Moreover, during the war years she still seems to have hoped that she might give birth to another child. That is the impression one takes from reading the letter she sent to her sister Anne in 1778 during the British occupation. Anne Francis had written to announce the arrival of one more child in her growing family, a daughter born at an especially inconvenient time, who would be named Elizabeth Powel Francis. She tried to console her sister by saying that her daughter should have more suitably been Elizabeth Powel's. "I feel a pre-Sentiment that my little unwellcome Name-sake," her sister replied, "will more than compensate for her unseasonable Visit; & if I shou'd prove a true

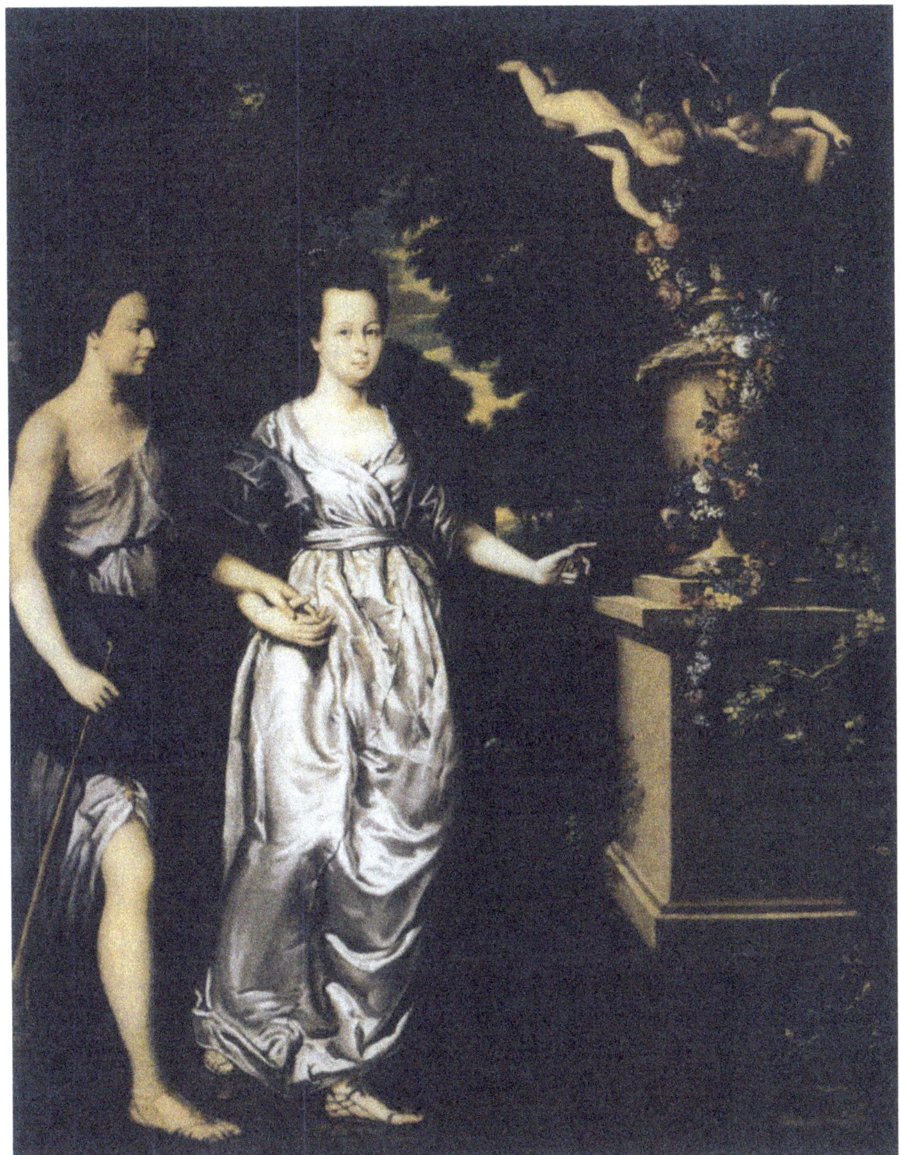

FIGURE 2. *Memorial to E. R.*, a mourning portrait painted by James Claypoole, Jr., signed and dated in Jamaica in 1774. Courtesy of the New Orleans Museum of Art.

Prophetess you will retract your generous wish of her being mine instead of yours."[118]

A date of about 1786 would also align the portrait in time with another full-sized study attributed to Matthew Pratt, that of Elizabeth Powel's mother.

The Pratt portrait of Ann Shippen Willing, thought to have been painted in the mid-1780s, about five years before her death, now hangs in the same room in the Powel House with her daughter's portrait. Then well into her seventies, Ann Willing showed no reluctance at that age to sit for her portrait as a bonneted matron, holding a book in her lap, whose figure amply fills the canvas (Figure 3).[119]

It would not have been unusual for two members of the same family to sit for the same artist at about the same time, especially if they were members of the Willing family and the artist was Matthew Pratt. According to Pratt's son Thomas, it was in this very period after the war that his father, discouraged by the weakened appreciation of the fine arts in Philadelphia, tried to revive his practice as a portrait painter. Both Elizabeth Powel and her mother were neighbors of Pratt's. As a widow, having been nudged out of the family mansion on Third Street, Ann Willing occupied a house on Pine Street, a short block away from where Pratt lived. If, in necessitous circumstances, Pratt decided to approach this source of prior patronage, he would have done so realizing that an artist was seldom called upon to paint the same subject a second time. Yet his familiarity with the Willing family and the commissions he had received in the past may have recommended him as a sympathetic interpreter of Elizabeth Powel's innermost feelings.[120]

Assuming that Pratt received what amounted to a double assignment, he nevertheless proceeded quite differently with his two subjects. Ann Willing, presented in an honest, straightforward manner, is shown wearing a voluminous dress and a shawl, clothing that seems authentically hers. By way of contrast, Elizabeth Powel's portrait has a didactic objective. To deliver the portrait's message as it was communicated to him, Matthew Pratt in all likelihood cut out of whole cloth the yellow dress that Elizabeth Powel, as bereaved mother, never owned and only wore in this painting. The dress Pratt thus assembled is much closer to a morning dress than to a mourning one, something in which he envisioned a mother of modesty might appear at the beginning of the day, but only in the presence of her husband and an infant child.[121] That dress, in a number of variations, can be found in other Pratt portraits: for example, the sawtooth cuffs are present in the portraits of Mrs. Benjamin West and Mrs. William Bradford, Jr., while the basic design of the dress, absent the steep décolletage, is repeated in the portraits of Mrs. Bradford and of Mrs. John Bush (Figure 4), both of them reliably dated in the period of the mid-1780s.[122]

The liberties Pratt felt his subject might take in the dress he designed for her to wear *en famille* could explain (but only partially so) the bewildering advice Thomas Jefferson imparted in 1783 to his eleven-year-old daughter, Martha: "Some ladies think they may under the privileges of the dishabille be loose and negligent of their dress in the morning. But be you from the moment you rise till you go to bed as cleanly and properly dressed as at the

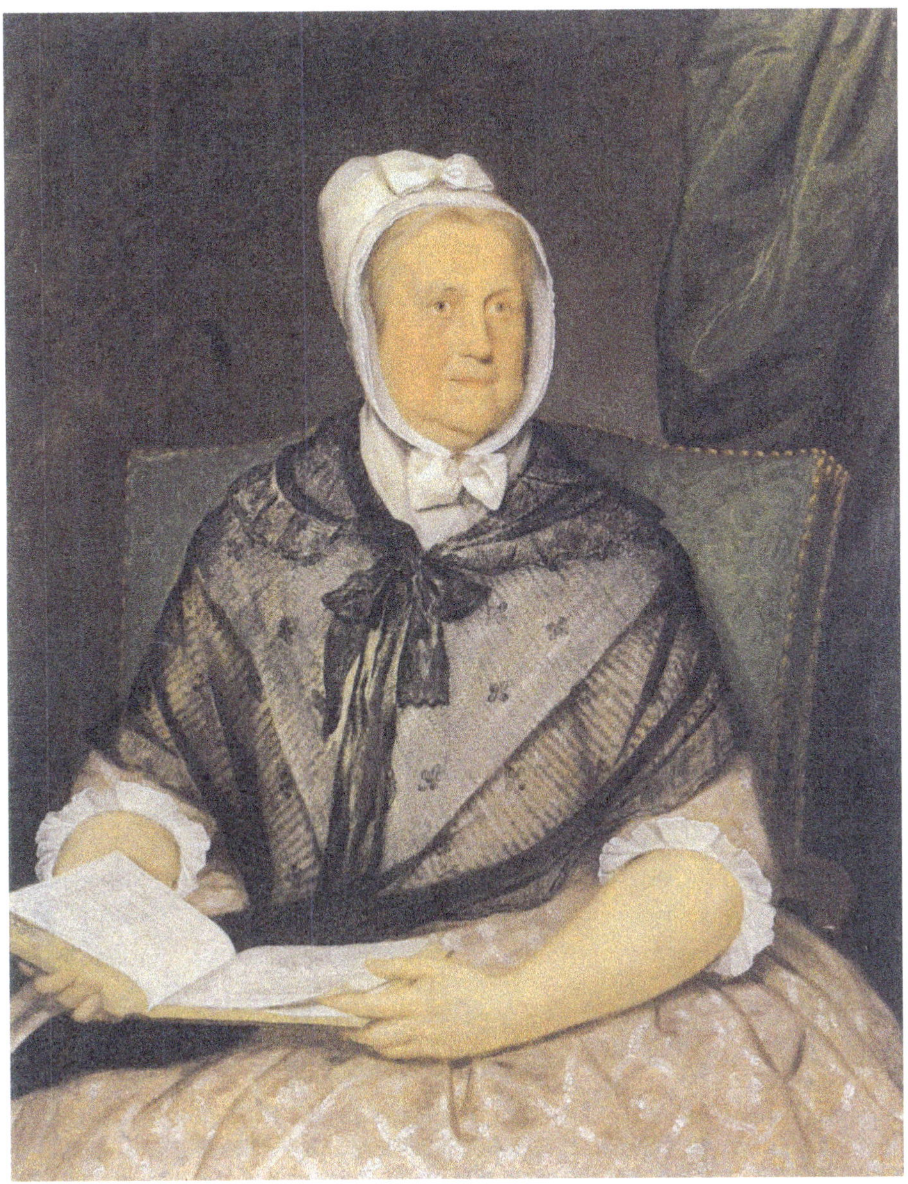

FIGURE 3. Portrait of Ann Shippen Willing, attributed to Matthew Pratt, circa 1786. Courtesy of the Philadelphia Society for the Preservation of Landmarks, Powel House.

hours of dinner or tea. A lady who has been seen as a sloven or slut in the morning, will never efface the impression she then made with all the dress and pageantry she can afterwards involve herself in."[123] That neither Matthew Pratt nor Elizabeth Powel provided the exact model of undress that so agitated Jefferson's thinking should not exclude an association of perspectives.

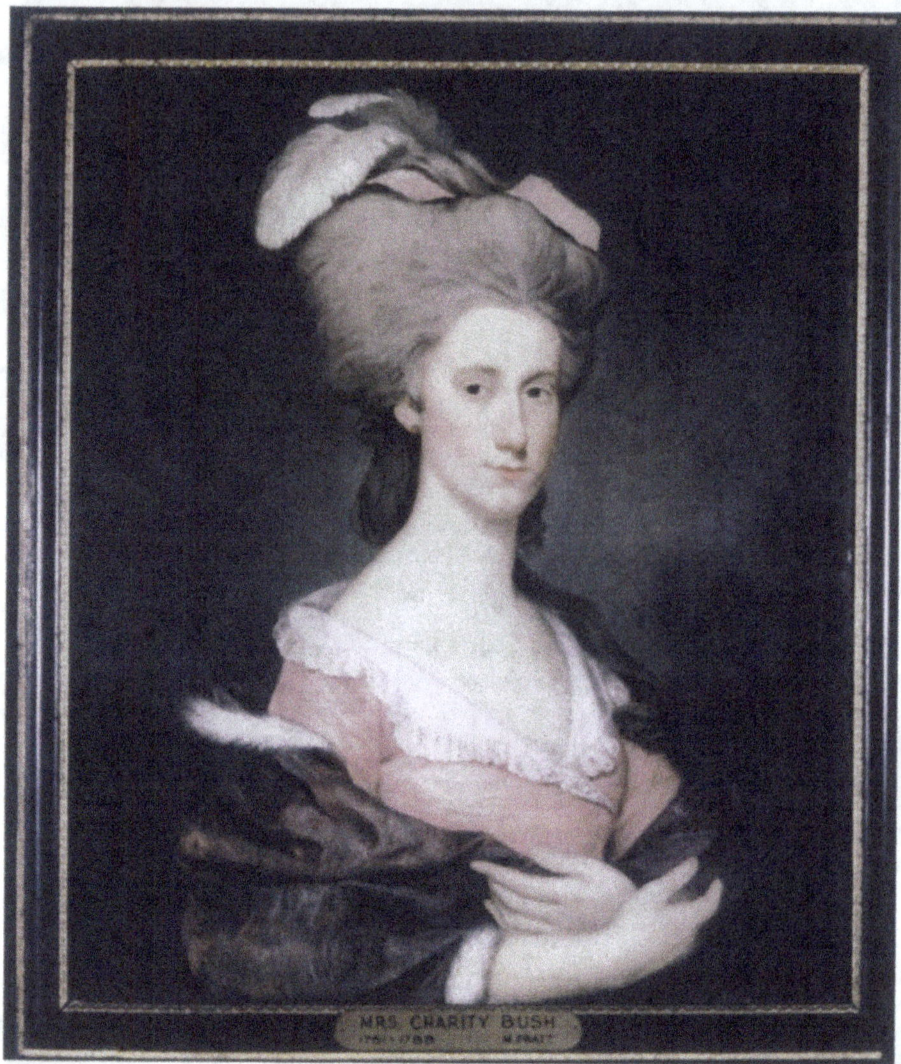

Figure 4. Portrait of Mrs. John Bush, attributed to Matthew Pratt, circa 1786, in which the subject wears an invented dress similar to that worn by Elizabeth Powel in the frontispiece portrait. Courtesy of the American Antiquarian Society.

Invented or fictional dress in portraiture was "a standard element of artistic practice in both America and England" during the eighteenth century, but one having, as Leslie Reinhardt has pointed out, a gender bias in that it was "a mode used almost exclusively for women." The characteristics of invented dress were, more often than not, "looseness and/or absence of stays; relative lack of pattern or ornament; and garment forms that were either structurally impossible or fundamentally different from prevailing fashion." The use of invented dress is conspicuous in the work of John Singleton Copley, a painter whom Pratt unequivocally admired and who, for a time, was mistakenly credited with the authorship of this portrait.[124]

Did Elizabeth Powel, as an essential collaborator in the production of her portrait, accept it without quibble once it was completed? Did it convey the message she intended, and did she find the yellow dress of Pratt's design fitting for that purpose? We know that she was far from uncritical in assessing artistic talent. In a letter to a friend in 1813, she declined the invitation to sit for her portrait by an aspiring young artist, in part because she wished to avoid offending "some of my nearest, and dearest Relatives" who had made similar requests of her that she had consistently turned down. But the more telling objection was her fear that "the young Gentleman is not sufficiently acquainted with the essential branch of his Profession" to do justice to his subject. The sample of his work that her friend had put before her failed to pass inspection, for, though she found recognizable the likeness of the person painted, "the colouring bore no resemblance to the fine natural complexion of the Original."[125]

In a recently published book of impressive scholarship, Margaretta Lovell contends that portraits of this period acted as powerful mnemonics, exciting "the bonds of affection but also, more important, those of duty." Portraits were thus typically painted to celebrate "the consecutiveness of the family line . . . at the time of an individual's achievement of majority, inheritance, marriage, or first issue." Serving such a purpose, they were hung in the principal rooms of the patron's house, where "they were observed by social and business visitors."[126]

Although Matthew Pratt's portrait of Elizabeth Powel also acted as a powerful mnemonic, it was decidedly not in celebration of the consecutiveness of the family line. Rather, as a means of recalling between husband and wife their pledge of love never to be fulfilled, it became a memorial to family discontinuity, to frustrated dynastic ambition. Nor can it be easily imagined that Elizabeth Powel would have permitted even close friends coming to the house on Third Street to view so personal an expression of grief. If she accepted the portrait as accurate narrative, composed in obedience to her wishes, she would nevertheless have insisted on hanging it in her and her husband's private apartments, located on the third floor of the Powel House, shielded from the gaze of the curious and from impertinent inquiry.

To summarize a blend of established fact and, one hopes, responsible conjecture, this portrait owned by the Pennsylvania Academy of the Fine Arts may be regarded, in a descending order of probability, as

- almost unquestionably the work of Matthew Pratt;
- a rare repeat commission—with Elizabeth Powel on this second occasion portrayed in mourning, as a bereaved mother and not as a grieving widow;
- showing its subject in invented dress that the artist thought appropriate for both a mother and a wife acknowledging the permanent loss of children to whom she could give birth;

- having a date more plausibly set in the mid-1780s than in about 1793; and
- intended for the purpose of private reminder and consolation, and not for viewing by others.

5

The Portrait's Missing Provenance

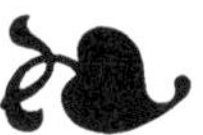

THERE IS A REMAINING QUESTION to confront, which, if it can be answered, may throw additional light on the preceding issues and the persuasiveness of their proposed resolution. That question is what happened to the painting in the long period prior to its acquisition by the academy in 1912. From whom and by what route did the portrait come to the academy? In short, how may that void of a century or more be filled and the portrait's missing provenance established? As a logical point of departure, we must resume following the portrait's subject, now in the closing decades of her life, for it was she, and she alone, who would have had control over its possession.

With the return of yellow fever a constant threat, Elizabeth Powel had no desire to stay in a district of its virulent impact close to the Delaware. In 1798 she sold the property on Third Street to William Bingham, the wealthy husband of her niece, who bought it for his daughter and son-in-law. That sale coincided with another devastating outbreak of yellow fever, claiming as one of its many victims Henry Hill, who had admired his neighbor so extravagantly at her fiftieth birthday party. She relocated for a brief interval to what would have seemed a safer place on the very outskirts of the settled city, between Tenth and Eleventh Streets on the north side of Market. By 1802 or thereabouts she changed her address once more, moving to a mansion on the north side of Chestnut Street, a short distance east of Seventh, which she would make her spacious home, surrounded by servants, until her death in 1830.[127] In self-imposed semiconfinement, she would be absorbed during those thirty years in not totally unrelated concerns about the future of her young country, about caring for and rewarding loyal servants, and about the welfare of her family whose members frequently competed for the favor of their wealthy relative.

Washington's death at the end of 1799 deprived her of a confidant and "inestimable friend," the guardian of America's destiny. In the absence of his tutelary authority, the success of the constitutional experiment became for her a more contingent calculation. By reason of her inherited wealth, she had a substantial stake in the stability of the new government. Her prejudices were solidly Federalist and Hamiltonian. As Jefferson was nearing the end of his second term, she asked her banker nephew whether, "at this momentous Crisis," investment in "the Six per Cent Stock of the U. States [meaning the Bank of the United States] . . . would be prudent," given that her primary object was to place "securely" the large sum she had at her disposal. She was scarcely reassured when the Federalist ticket lost the election in 1808 and she was forced to contemplate "Mr. Madison . . . as the President of these U. States of America."[128]

When, however, by Congress's formal declaration, the War of 1812 began, she put domestic politics aside and became fiercely partisan in her country's defense. If any doubt might linger that at least one patriot occupied the house on Third Street during the Revolution, her reaction against this second attack on American independence should put such doubt to rest. In summoning the past as witness, she went so far as to analogize Britain's slash-and-burn conduct of this war to its suppression of Scottish independence in the Jacobite rebellion of 1745, an unexpected parallel for someone to draw who had an engrained suspicion of any cause having a Catholic tinge to it:

> During the revolutionary War I had an opportunity of seeing some of the finest, and best appointed armies of Europe, and I am of the opinion that their common Soldiers cannot with truth be put in comparison with those of our Country whether in Person weight of character, or any other valuable property of rational Man. . . . The Armies of Europe are mostly composed of the refuse of our Species, even the Officers are generally (particularly the English with a few exceptions) Men of desperate fortunes or the younger Sons of genteel families, who are glad to get rid of the expense, and trouble of weak immoral dissipated lazy Boys, that are utterly incapable of providing for themselves in any line of productive industry. Certainly the English are a proud, cruel sordid tyrannic selfish Nation, as they have evinced by their brutal conduct in Asia, Africa, America, Ireland, Denmark, and in Scotland in the year 45 when they did what they have the insolence to threaten to do to us, and this avowedly under the sanction of their Government. . . . I cannot but suspect from the present conduct of the British, that they are fast returning to their pristine state of barbarity. Their execrable practice of pillaging, and burning, is only worthy of a Nation of Incendiaries, and thieves of the worst Cast. Contrast what I have alledged [*sic*] as strictly true, with the real pretensions of the American Army, which is generally composed of the Yeomanry of our Country, respectable citizens, industrious well informed Tradesmen who have families and Property to protect, Professional Men of various descriptions, and some highminded generous Gentlemen of independent Fortune [who], although they are not designated by Titular distinctions, have just claims to great personal Nobility.

It is perhaps worth noting that the letter containing this outburst was dated January 30, 1815, five weeks after the belligerents had signed the peace treaty at Ghent on Christmas Eve but two weeks before that news reached America, even though the formal ending of the war would not necessarily have brought about the cessation of Elizabeth Powel's hostility.[129]

As a widow, Elizabeth Powel reached out in gratitude, even more so than previously, to those who were of service to her. David Gray was an all-purpose carpenter who may have built her new house on Chestnut Street, who was responsible for enlarging the farmhouse at Powelton to a mansion, and who was generally on call whenever she needed his help. In her will she left him a generous bequest of five hundred dollars. In 1808, she sent to David Gray's wife, "as an evidence of her gratitude to Mr. Gray for his unwearied and faithful attention to her accommodation and interest in the care of her real estate," a glass for the mantelpiece. It was accompanied by the volunteered advice that "Mrs. Gray may with propriety either suspend the Glass perpendicularly in the French fashion, or put it across the Chimney in the American manner as is most appropriate to her taste."[130]

But it was her household staff she was more attentive to, and dependent on. In the thirty years before she died, the composition of that staff inevitably changed, not only because of the passage of time but also because of the varying capabilities of the people she employed, including some outright disappointments. By and large, however, she was able to count on faithful servants to stay with her. One such servant was Ennels Cork, "a bound black boy," who, she directed her lawyer in 1811, should be given "whatever may remain of his time at my decease, to be disposed of by his Parents Samuel & Elizabeth Cork as they may think most advantageous for their Child." While still a youngster, his mistress entered him "as a half day Scholar . . . from 3 to 5 oclock in the Afternoon at the School of Mr. James Kelly (where he heretofore made a very good progress in those parts of Education that he was instructed in) . . . to be taught Spelling reading writing, and Arithmetick," adding only her request that Mr. Kelly oblige "by directing Ennels Cork to return home every day immediately on his dismission from his school." Ennels Cork remained in Elizabeth Powel's service until her death in 1830. Under her will, he received a lifetime annuity of fifty dollars that he would collect for many years, being the last to die of the several annuitants mentioned in her will.[131]

Her servants had thus become companions for whom she accepted personal responsibility. When her household was hit with the flu in the fall of 1815, she applied to Dr. Adam Kuhn, the physician in whose judgment she placed the greatest trust, for advice "respecting the mode of treatment most proper to be pursued with my Domesticks, who with one exception are all under the distressing influence of Influenza." Dr. Kuhn, then old and infirm, had retired from the practice of medicine; a stern critic of Benjamin Rush's aggressive treatment of yellow fever, he preferred more gentle remedies than bleeding and purgatives. If he replied to Mrs. Powel, he may have prescribed nothing other than bed rest and chicken soup for her domestics in distress, as a dozen years before, when Elizabeth Drinker complained of similar flu-like symptoms, he recommended she take "broath made of a Partridge."[132]

With more than one valued black servant in her employ, Elizabeth Powel took a fervent stand against slavery. She had grown up in a household where slaves were present, and at the outset of their marriage, as we have seen, Samuel Powel owned slaves. Whether on moral grounds or because of the growing supply of more reliable free labor, Samuel Powel appears at an early date to have divested himself of the few slaves he had. In 1780 the Pennsylvania legislature passed a limited emancipation act, the first adopted in the former colonies, while at about the same time the Pennsylvania Abolition Society mounted an attack in principle on the institution of slavery. In exercising his customary caution not to anticipate the outcome of any campaign for fundamental change, Samuel Powel was not among those who joined the Pennsylvania Abolition Society.[133]

Had Elizabeth Powel wished herself to be a member, she would have been turned down because of her sex. In any case, her attitude toward slavery probably evolved, ending in full-blown opposition only after she shook free from her husband's prudential constraints. That she subscribed, however, sooner rather than later, to the goals of the Pennsylvania Abolition Society may be deduced from the minutes of a special meeting the society called three months after her death:

> On Motion: the following extract from the last Will & testament of the late Elizabeth Powell is directed to be placed in our minutes . . . viz:
>
> "Whereas I abhor Slavery under any modification and consider the practice of holding our fellow creatures in bondage alike inconsistent with the principles of humanity and the free republic institutions.
>
> "And Whereas I feel it to be the duty of every individual to co-operate by all honourable means in the Abolition of Slavery, & in the restoration of freedom to that important part of the family of mankind, which has so long groaned under oppression.
>
> "I do therefore hereby give and bequeath to the Penna. Society for promoting the Abolition of Slavery &tc an annuity of one hundred Dollars for and during the term of twenty years to commence one year after my Decease."

The feeling of abhorrence she so strongly expressed originated long before 1819, the year in which she signed her will containing these provisions. She had been mulling over the terms of this particular gift for some time, with the result that the language quoted in the society's minutes was distinctively of her own composition. In 1814, as she was considering this bequest, she confidently predicted to her lawyer that "the understanding of my Countrymen will be so illuminated" that the institution of slavery would disappear in the United States before the annual gift she proposed ran out.[134]

By far Elizabeth Powel's greatest concern during this period was preserving the Powel family name and reputation. She staked her every hope on her nephew John, who, in his serial romantic entanglements, succeeded in driving her to complete distraction. Lecture followed lecture, yet all, it seemed, to no avail. After he had gone abroad in 1808, she reminded him of the dual purpose of this trip: "The principal object of your voyage," she wrote, "was the attainment of knowledge in the useful, as well as the ornamental pursuits of life, and to disengage your mind from disagreeable embarrassment that from precipitancy, and inexperience you had unfortunately plunged into." In this last statement, she was referring obliquely to what she specifically disclosed to an inquisitive niece: the embarrassment was John's engagement "when he was a Boy of eighteen with a fascinating Woman of at least twenty three years," a match that both his parents and his aunt opposed as "so very inadequate to his pretensions."

To her despair, her nephew again succumbed while abroad. Expecting to marry, he requested his aunt to convert by present gift much of the legacy he looked forward to receiving upon her death. She cautioned him, "as a Man of delicacy and honour," that he must abandon "every thought of Marriage" until by his exertions he was "in a capacity to give comfortable maintenance to a family." To drive that point home, she added, "[h]ad my sons lived they would have been educated for some profitable Profession . . . [as] my Ancestors and those of my Husband were all industriously employed in some lucrative pursuit." The request for a present gift in lieu of a legacy she flatly rejected: " . . . I never mean to divest myself of my Estate during my life. At my death you will comfortably be possessed of a handsome proportion of my Property. If it is then mine to give."[135]

That underscored proviso was meant to spur her nephew to more responsible conduct because Elizabeth Powel had every intention of continuing to manage her wealth while using the prospective dispositions in her will as instruments of persuasion. Nor did her nephew have any doubt concerning what his aunt was aiming to achieve or the effect her tactics had on his own thinking. He wrote years later in a memoir for his children: "Notwithstanding her attachment to me, and the conviction which she conveyed to my mind, that I was to be the heir of her fortune, she endeavored most sedulously to convey to the other members of her family that it was a prize, for which all or any might contend."[136]

John Hare Powel, as he was then known, put everything at risk when he fell in love with the granddaughter of Charles Carroll of Carrollton, a signer of the Declaration of Independence, a wealthy Marylander, and a Roman Catholic. Elizabeth Caton was one of three sisters of overpowering charm, hailed as "The Three Graces," each of whom would eventually marry into the British aristocracy. John Powel's infatuation with her reached a crisis stage in the summer of 1814 when his aunt foresaw the necessity of disinheriting him. To his friend Thomas Cadwalader, she confided that John Powel "has evinced himself a very Child on the subject of my Sex." It was bad enough that he was bewitched by "a perfidious Siren," a "faithless Gypsy," "a paltry Girl," "a mere Pageant of a Ball Room." What disturbed his aunt even more was Elizabeth Caton's religion and the prospect that, as a Catholic, she would entice into an alliance "the Man that I had selected to transmit the Name of the virtuous correct Protestant Powel to Posterity." Broadminded though she liked to think herself, Elizabeth Powel drew the line when it came to the pope in Rome and the Catholic faith. "I most solemnly assured him," she recorded in a long memorandum about the battle she waged, "that the Estate of the modest virtuous protestant Powel should not by any agency of mine be transmitted to any Descendant of Charles Carroll of Carrollton. And to this declaration I will most solemnly adhere, by altering my Will." The acute danger passed, either because her nephew folded under unremitting pressure or because the temptress in Baltimore decided to focus her charm elsewhere. John Powel returned to Philadelphia, and Elizabeth Caton went on several years later to marry in the church of St. Roche in Paris Sir George William Jenningham, the 8th Baron Stafford.[137]

Her nephew's erratic conduct, as well as the many claims on her generosity, made settling on the provisions in her will an extended exercise for Elizabeth Powel and her lawyer. In fact, she probably executed two or more wills before the final one. For a long period during the second decade of the nineteenth century, both by letter and in personal interviews, she was in constant consultation with Edward S. Burd, a Shippen cousin, about her will and the gifts she was considering.[138] The document that emerged at last, which she signed on May 22, 1819, ran to forty-nine pages of a clerk's handwriting. At the bottom of each page the testatrix placed her signature for verification purposes—in itself a considerable labor. This will, superseding all prior wills, would be supplemented by four codicils, one executed in 1820 and three others in 1824. Because of the extended list of people and causes that Elizabeth Powel wished to benefit, her will, in its entirety, including the codicils, is a challenge to wade through.[139]

Nowhere in this will or in the codicils is there a specific reference to the Pratt portrait. Yet Elizabeth Powel took great care to make gifts of her possessions that had particular sentimental value. Thus, she left a "silver chafindish [*sic*] . . . formerly the property of my Great Grandfather Edward Shippen," to her great-nephew Charles Willing; her "bracelets with my mother's hair and Mr. Powel's set with brilliants," to her great-niece Mary Page; her "brilliant mourning urn ring, containing the hair of my Youngest Son," to her niece Martha Hare; "the miniature likeness of my Sister Francis, taken shortly previous to her death," to her great-niece Anne Francis; her "brilliant mourning urn ring, containing the hair of my eldest Son—as a testimony of affection," to her niece Mary Clymer; "the miniature likeness of his father," to her friend and lawyer Edward Shippen Burd; the portrait of his grandmother "my Dear Sister Stirling," to her great-nephew John Stirling, "knowing that it would be particularly agreeable to him to possess it"; and, in one of numerous gifts she made outside her family, "my large Silver cream jug of American manufacture, a specimen of good taste, so congenial with her nature," to her "amiable neighbor Mrs. William Waln."[140]

After these specific bequests and generous pecuniary legacies for friends, relatives, and servants (often taking the form of a stipulated annual payment or annuity), John Hare Powel received the bulk of her estate, but not without strings attached. She entailed her real estate by restricting its ownership through successive generations on the condition, as long as it could be legally enforced, that the beneficiary would be a male bearing the Powel name. Her nephew later explained this testamentary plan to his family: "Her intention was evident, she meant her name to be supported by her fortune, for, in the event of failure of male issue, my daughter could, in no event, inherit under the will." No such restriction applied, however, nor could it, to her personal property, which, subject to all these gifts she made to others in her will, she left outright to her nephew. Therefore, if she had not disposed of the Pratt portrait in the will or by gift during her lifetime, John Hare Powel would have acquired it under one or another residuary clause in her will.[141]

In spite of the ability she demonstrated to leave items of sentimental value to appreciative members of her family, Elizabeth Powel would have faced a real dilemma in attempting to leave the portrait by specific bequest. What words were then available to express, so long after the event, the grief that touched her deeply and that Pratt was commissioned to portray? It would have been, we may sympathize, an emotionally difficult yet not impossible task. Had she provided, for example, something like the following, much of the mystery concerning her portrait would have disappeared: "I give to ________ the portrait of myself painted by Matthew Pratt in about 1786 that bears witness to the sorrow my husband and I shared in the loss of our beloved offspring." Yet, failing such precision, it seems inconceivable that she would have allowed the portrait to pass by default to her nephew, the expedient substitute for the children she had lost in infancy.[142] Instead, she would have sought to entrust the painting to someone who would understand the reason for the sadness that infused her image. That person was her housekeeper and close friend, a widow like herself but with children left to raise, Amy Roberts.[143]

Elizabeth Powel did not include Amy Roberts among her loyal servants and beneficiaries in the will she first signed in 1795 nor in 1800 when it was republished with certain interlineated changes. She referred for the first time in late 1800 to "Mrs. Roberts" being in her employ. By 1808 this servant had become "My good and faithfull Amy," to whom early one morning, while outside Philadelphia, Elizabeth Powel dispatched detailed instructions concerning a dinner party her nephew intended to give the following evening in his aunt's grand house on Chestnut Street. By then it was clear that Amy, having full authority over the other members of the staff, could be counted on to produce the cook's specialty of "Calves Head Turtle Soup," to decant fine wine in advance of the meal, and to rotate china and table linen as the several courses were served.[144]

As Amy's mistress pondered the provisions in her new will, she returned repeatedly in correspondence with Edward S. Burd to the debt she owed in "gratitude and affection to my humble efficient friend and Housekeeper Amy

Roberts." So worrisome did Margaret Hare, the mother of the favored nephew, find this attachment to Amy Roberts that Elizabeth Powel thought it necessary to supply this assurance at the end of a message to her sister: "Mrs. Roberts begs to be affectionately remembered to you all. Indeed she has been a sincere friend to you and all your Children, and to my happiness she is all important."[145]

Elizabeth Powel's family needlessly worried about the housekeeper's undue influence. In her will she was very generous, but not disproportionately so, to this servant who had become indispensable to her, both as a household manager and as a friend in whom she could freely confide. She gave Amy an annuity for her remaining lifetime of one hundred pounds, "Pennsylvania currency," as well as two thousand dollars "to be paid her in three years after my Decease to enable her to pursue any business that may be agreeable to her." Each of Amy's two children received fifty dollars, one of whom, a daughter named Maria, had married John Murphy and named her first child Elizabeth Powel Murphy. Amy Roberts was given all the furniture "of her present chamber, including bed, bedding, etc.," on the third floor of the Chestnut Street mansion as well as the furniture in the north chamber of the second floor, most of the china in the house, a small silver teapot and porringer, a small copper sauce pan lined with silver, and Elizabeth Powel's "best velvet Cloak lined with Fur." The common table linen and sheeting, pillows, and bolster cases were to be divided equally between Amy and Elizabeth's niece Ann Willing. Finally, to Amy fell the special responsibilities of deciding which of her mistress's clothes should be distributed to the poor and of supervising the members of the household staff kept on regular wages for a period after the death of Elizabeth Powel. At the end, no one could claim a closer, a more intimate connection with the decedent than her faithful housekeeper.[146]

Immediately after the funeral service and her burial, the interested parties assembled at the house on Chestnut Street for the reading of the will, all forty-nine pages of it. Rumblings of discontent were heard then and in the weeks to follow. According to Deborah Logan, the formidable Quaker diarist, the Griffitts, members of Samuel Powel's own family, made "a loud clamour" at the diversion of so much Powel wealth to the favored nephew. Inclined toward the Griffitts, who were good Quakers, Logan remarked that the "the Ancestors of the Powels were a succession of industrious penurious persons, who worked incessantly at accumulation—it would now seem to the unwelcome purpose of enriching other peoples' heirs." She passed on gossip: "John Hare [Powel] and all his family are preparing to go to Europe in a month or two, to spend his money (as much as he can come at), and his stiff-starched Sister is going with him."[147]

Especially because of the number of specific bequests, the executors lost no time in ordering an inventory or appraisement of Elizabeth Powel's personal property. Schedule No. 2 of the inventory they obtained is an itemized list of values assigned, room by room, to "Furniture Wines etc. in the late dwelling house of Elizabeth Powel in Chestnut St . . . at the time of her decease." Unfortunately, the appraiser used generic descriptions rather than specific ones, referring, for example, to "pictures" found in several rooms. The only time he identifies "paintings," as distinguished from "pictures," is when he inventories the contents of the northwest room on the second floor, all of which (other than two excluded pieces of furniture) it would appear from her will Elizabeth Powel intended to give to her housekeeper. One way or the other, either through these unspecific but inclusive provisions in her will or by a gift completed during her lifetime, she made certain that Amy Roberts would take custody of the portrait Matthew Pratt had painted.[148]

This loyal servant and friend died in October 1844 at the age of seventy, as noted in the records of the cemetery in which she was buried.[149] At the time of her death she was living with her son, William D. Roberts, an upholsterer, in a house that she owned at 35 Dean Street (later South Camac Street), between Locust and Spruce. In that same block of Dean Street she owned another house that her daughter Maria and Maria's husband, John K. Murphy, occupied.[150] From a condition of impoverishment when her husband died many years before, Amy Roberts had accumulated sufficient property and family concerns to cause her to consult an attorney and to leave a will of her own. Providing separately for her daughter and her son, she also made gifts to her three Murphy grandchildren. Among other provisions for her daughter Maria, she gave her "my Jet Brest Pin containing the hair of my departed Friend Madam Powell [*sic*]." To her granddaughter Elizabeth Powell (also misspelled in the will) Murphy, who would soon acquire the married name of Kern, she bequeathed "all the Furniture in my Bed chamber." Although the inventory and appraisement subsequently made in this estate failed to locate particular articles in particular rooms, it did value at five dollars the one "oil painting" owned by the decedent. Was this not therefore the Pratt portrait that Amy Roberts kept close to her as a powerful memento and that she finally parted with when in her will, perhaps following a prior example, she transferred "all the Furniture in my Bed chamber" to her mistress's namesake?[151]

A gap remains between the presumed testamentary gift of the portrait to Amy Roberts's granddaughter and its acquisition by Robert M. Lindsay, an antiquarian book seller, an occasional publisher, and an art dealer.[152] How long did Elizabeth Powel Murphy Kern keep it, and did she dispose of it before her own death whenever that occurred? Though she was born sometime between 1820 and 1824, she could have retained at most only a faint recollection of that formidable woman whose name she bore. Lindsay may have acquired the portrait on the cheap and held it in stock for a considerable time. In any event, it reappeared in 1906 as a painting that he offered for sale as the work of Charles Willson Peale at a price of thirty-five hundred dollars.

That it was then available for purchase was confirmed in a genealogical study of the Hare-Powel families whose diligent author-compiler traced its possession back to Amy Roberts. Three year later, when the Powel House was threatened with demolition, Philadelphia newspapers sounded the alarm and ran stories about the Powels and their high style of living. In one such article there appeared a photograph of this portrait, which Lindsay had then relabeled the work of John Singleton Copley.[153]

Charles Henry Hart, who weighed in so heavily after the Pennsylvania Academy of the Fine Arts acquired the portrait in 1912, had more to say on this subject in another letter he sent to the editor of the *American Art News*: "As to the so-called Copley being a portrait of Eliza Willing Powel, there is nothing but the tradition of servants' kitchen gossip to vouch for it, and every one can measure the value of that kind of verification." The canvas, according to Hart, had been "hawked about by different dealers for the last five years." Although several times asked to provide a positive opinion in support of its claimed "authorship and subject," he had, he insisted, steadfastly refused to do so.[154] On the issue of authorship, instead of emphatically pronouncing it the work of James Peale, he would have done better to recall his own words from a judicious essay published on Matthew Pratt twenty years earlier: "[Pratt's] name is strangely unfamiliar where it should be well known, and scores of ancestral portraits, at least among those in the Middle States, cherished as the work of John Singleton Copley or of others equally noted, came doubtless from the easel of Pratt."[154] On the issue of whether Elizabeth Willing Powel was the subject of the portrait, an identification that he disputed, he would have proved himself the more responsible art historian and critic had he actually measured the value of "servants' kitchen gossip." That gossip, still audible from the past, would have verified the painting as a portrait of Elizabeth Powel and helped to decipher its message of lasting personal grief.

Epilogue

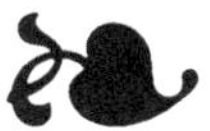

WHEN SHE WAS EIGHTY-ONE or eighty-two, at about the time Lafayette returned to America on a triumphal tour, Elizabeth Powel consented to sit for her portrait (Figure 5). Who or what persuaded her to do this, the record does not disclose. The artist was a young, largely unknown painter from Connecticut named Francis Alexander, the kind of beginner in the trade for whom she had refused to sit some years before.[156] In allowing herself to be portrayed at this stage in her life, she may have simply recalled the example her mother provided on a similar occasion when Pratt painted her in her old age.

In late September 1824, the procession of welcome for Lafayette wound its way through Philadelphia, certainly the place, more than anywhere else, that would rekindle for him memories of participating in America's Revolution. The managers of this event had planned that in its final stretch the parade would progress eastward on Chestnut Street to the State House, pausing before the mansion of an old friend of the honored hero. We cannot be sure whether, then or in the festivities that followed, Lafayette once again encountered Elizabeth Powel.[157] Perhaps he sought her out in a private interview, more in keeping with her own wishes. If they met, he might well have seen her as Francis Alexander has pictured her with unsparing accuracy, in this nimbus of lace, wrinkles and all.[158]

The same prominent features that appear in the Alexander portrait were present in the two portraits Matthew Pratt painted long before, first of a young woman about to embark on marriage and then of a mother in mourning for her lost sons. What is particularly striking about this portrayal is the intensity of Elizabeth Powel's engagement with the observer. It is as if, no longer separated at a distance from us, she has contrived this means of delivering one last message. "Here I am," she seems to say, "old and rheumatic, having lived a long life full of challenges. Yet I have persevered."

Her own words, however, not invented ones, will more appropriately serve as summation for the life of a remarkable woman. Thus she acknowledged the birthday wishes of her brother several years earlier: "I have certainly experienced severe trials, and some hard dispensations of Providence. . . . To travel with some dignity, innocence, and usefulness, down the Road which leads from the Morning of Youth to the Night of the Grave, is perhaps as much as we can flatter ourselves with accomplishing."[159]

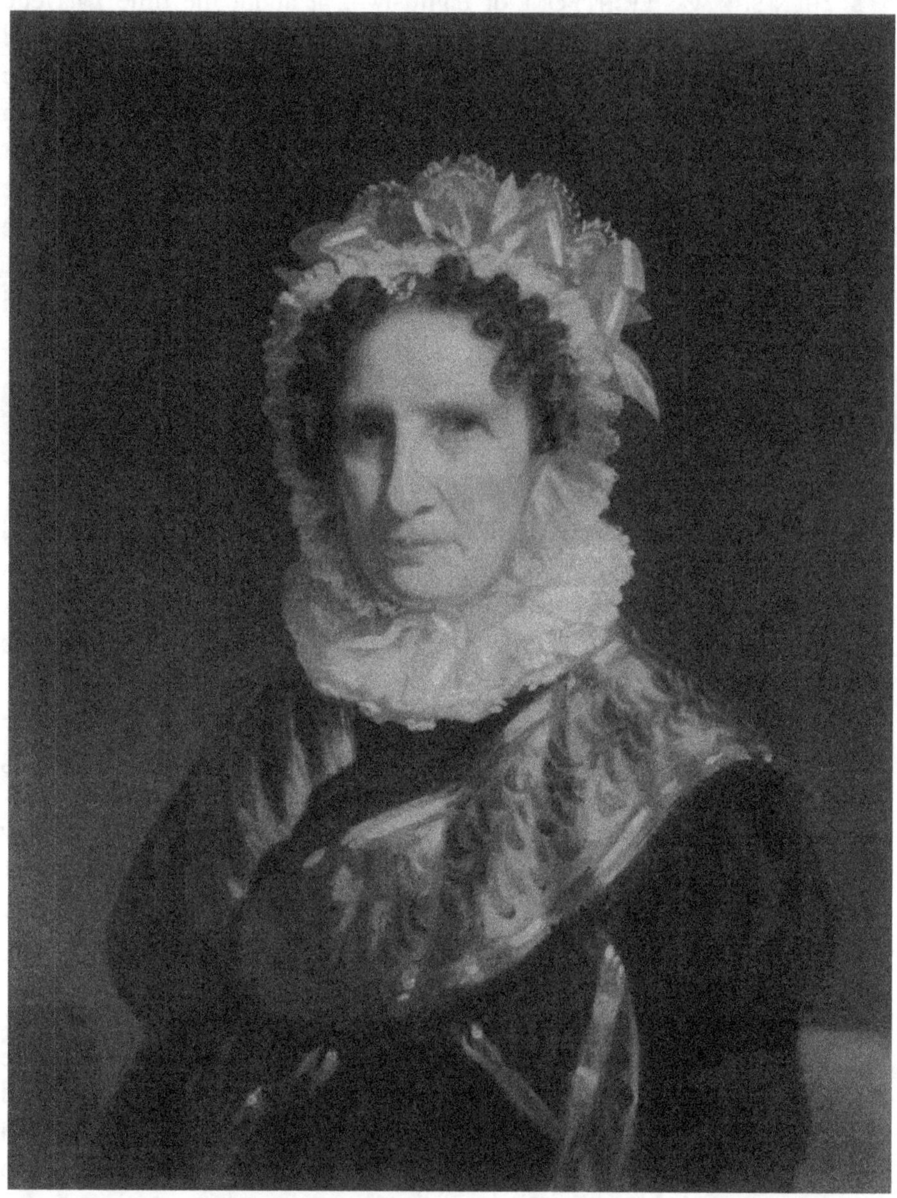

Figure 5. Portrait of Madam Powel (Elizabeth Powel), by Francis Alexander, circa 1825. Courtesy of the Museum of Fine Arts, Boston. Bequest of Pauline L. Dolliver. Photograph © 2006 Musuem of Fine Arts, Boston.

Notes

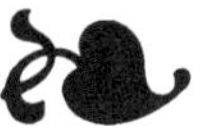

1. The canvas measures 39³/16-by-32¹/16 inches. For these dimensions and other information concerning the painting and its conservation, see the registrar's file for the portrait at the Pennsylvania Academy of the Fine Arts, Philadelphia, PA (hereafter cited as PAFA). For general background on eighteenth-century American portraiture, see Margaretta M. Lovell, *Art in a Season of Revolution: Painters, Artisans, and Patrons in Early America* (Philadelphia: University of Pennsylvania Press, 2005); the several perceptive contributions in Ellen G. Miles, ed., *The Portrait in Eighteenth-Century America* (Newark, DE: University of Delaware Press, 1993); Richard H. Saunders and Ellen G. Miles, *American Colonial Portraits, 1700–1776* (Washington, DC: Smithsonian Institution Press, 1987); and Carrie Rebora and Paul Staiti, Erica E. Hirshler, Theodore E. Stebbins, Jr., and Carol Troyen, *John Singleton Copley in America* (New York: The Metropolitan Museum of Art, 1995). As for stays and their absence, see Claudia Brush Kidwell, "Are Those Clothes Real? Transforming the Way Eighteenth-Century Portraits are Studied," *Dress* 24 (1997), 8–10; and Leslie Reinhardt, " 'The Work of Fancy and Taste': Copley's Invented Dress and the Case of Rebecca Boylston," *Dress* 29 (2003): 4, 12, 14.

2. The portrait's description is based on William Sawitzky, *Matthew Pratt, 1734–1805* (New York: The New-York Historical Society, 1942), 61–62.

3. For the symbols and conventions of mourning in eighteenth-century America, see Linda Baumgarten, *What Clothes Reveal: The Language of Clothing in Colonial and Federal America* (Williamsburg, VA: Colonial Williamsburg Foundation, 2002), 176–81; Robin Jaffee Frank, *Love and Loss: American Portrait and Mourning Miniatures* (New Haven: Yale University Press, 2000); Anita Schorsch, *Mourning Becomes America: Mourning Art in the New Nation* (Clinton, NJ: Main Street Press, 1976), and Schorsch, "Key to the Kingdom: The Iconography of a Mourning Picture," *Winterthur Portfolio* 14 (1979): 41–71; Nancy Schrom Dye and Daniel Blake Smith, "Mother Love and Infant Death, 1750–1920," *Journal of American History* 73 (Sept. 1986): 329–53; and Mary V. Thompson, "The Lowest Ebb of Misery: Death and Mourning in the Family of George Washington," *Historic Alexandria Quarterly* (Spring 2001): 1–14.

4. George B. Tatum, *Philadelphia Georgian: The City House of Samuel Powel and Some of its Neighbors* (Middletown, CT: Wesleyan University Press, 1976), 26. Tatum's work remains the indispensable starting point for an appreciation of Samuel Powel and the Powel House. Tatum speculates inconsistently that the portrait might also have been painted in celebration of Elizabeth Powel's fiftieth birthday that occurred in 1793. Ibid., 24–25. An interpretation of the portrait, as tied to the death of Samuel Powel, is advanced by the editor of François-Jean, Marquis de Chastellux, *Travels in North America in the Years 1780, 1781 and 1782*, rev. trans. and ed. Howard C. Rice, Jr. (Chapel Hill: University of North Carolina Press, 1963), 1:301–302 n. 29. See also James Thomas Flexner, *George Washington and the New Nation (1783–1793)* (Boston: Little, Brown and Company, 1970), 321.

5. Diaries of Deborah Norris Logan, Historical Society of Pennsylvania, Philadelphia, PA (the Society hereafter cited as HSP), vol. 12, pp. 239–40, 265. A recent evaluation of Deborah Logan and her reliability as a witness may be found in Susan M. Stabile, *Memory's Daughters: The Material Culture of Remembrance in Eighteenth-Century America* (Ithaca: Cornell University Press, 2004); see also Terri L. Premo, " 'Like a Being Who Does Not Belong': The Old Age of Deborah Norris Logan," *Pennsylvania Magazine of History and Biography* (hereafter cited as PMHB) 107 (1983): 85–112.

6. Edward L. Clark, comp., *Record of Inscriptions on the Tablets and Grave-Stones in the Burial-Grounds of Christ Church, Philadelphia* (Philadelphia: Collins, 1864), 129. Lavish tribute was paid the deceased in *Poulson's American Daily Advertiser*, Feb. 26, 1830, where the anonymous eulogist lauded her "extraordinary endowments," her mind "in a mould of unusual strength and fine proportions," her manner and sentiments as having "all the graces of feminine delicacy," her connection with the leading actors in the struggle for independence, the "elevated direction to her conversation and reflections," her ability to draw around her "the young and the gay," her "active and unwearied benevolence," and her "deep and settled aversion to slavery."

7. The primary source of Elizabeth Powel's correspondence is the Powel Family Papers (Collection 1582) at HSP (the Papers, hereafter cited as PFP). Almost all of her letters are copies she made of the originals, and whenever letters of hers from PFP are herein cited, they will be such copies unless otherwise indicated. Elizabeth Powel's letters as actually received may be found in the George Washington Papers at the Library of Congress's "American Memory" (accessible online at http://memory.loc.gov/ammem/html) and in the Martha Washington Papers at Mount Vernon. There is virtually nothing in her hand at HSP or elsewhere for the period from 1820 to her death in 1830. As early as 1808, her sister Anne Francis wrote that "Sister Powel . . . -never has Considered herself quite Well, and often Confines herself to her Chamber. . . . She is certainly Rheumatick." Anne Francis to Mary Byrd, Mar. 19, 1808, *Virginia Magazine of History and Biography* 54 (1946): 117.

8. Board minutes, May 23 and June 3, 1912, PAFA Archives.

9. Charles Henry Hart to Editor of *American Art News*, Aug. 10, 1915, in Charles Henry Hart, Scrapbook, 1909–1915, PAFA Archives.

10. See Richard H. Saunders, "The Eighteenth-Century Portrait in American Culture of the Nineteenth and Twentieth Centuries," in Miles, ed., *Portrait in Eighteenth-Century America*, 138–52. Then in good odor at the Academy and as chairman of its Committee on Exhibitions, Hart wrote the introduction to the catalogue for the 1887–1888 exhibition: *Loan Exhibition of Historical Portraits, December 1, 1887–January 15, 1888* (Philadelphia: Globe Printing House, 1887).

11. Letter to Director of New-York Historical Society, May 26, 1942 (copy), portrait file, Registrar, PAFA.

12. Sawitzky, *Matthew Pratt*, 7–14.

13. During the colonial period, the practice of signing portraits was just emerging among upscale painters as a means of attracting customers, whereas going on a "painting tour" was a generally adopted strategy for drumming up trade, if not pursued to quite the same extent that Pratt did prior to the Revolution. See Lovell, *Art in a Season of Revolution, 14, 40, 60–61*; and Jessie Porsch, " 'In Just Lines to Trace'—the Colonial Artist, 1700–1776," in Miles, ed., *Portrait in Eighteenth-Century America*, 63.

14. "Autobiographical Notes of Matthew Pratt, Painter," PMHB 19 (1896): 460–61. The original notes left by Pratt, as supplemented by information his son Thomas supplied, were lost, but not before a copy was made and donated to HSP by the ubiquitous Charles Henry Hart. Sawitzky republished this material verbatim in his *Matthew Pratt*, 17–24. For further biographical detail about Pratt, see Matthew Baigell, *Dictionary of American Art* (New York: Harper & Row, 1979), 288–89; Saunders and Miles, *American Colonial Portraits, 265–68;* William Dunlap, *A History of the Rise and Progress of the Arts of Design in the United States*, rev. ed. (1834; repr., New York: Dover Publications, Inc., 1969), 1:98–103; and John Caldwell and Oswaldo

Rodriguez Roque, *American Paintings in the Metropolitan Museum of Art* (New York: Metropolitan Museum of Art in Association with Princeton University Press, 1994), 1:55–63.

15. "Autobiographical Notes of Pratt," 461–62. The accomplishment represented by *The American School* is thoroughly analyzed in Susan Rather, "A Painter's Progress: Matthew Pratt and *The American School*," *Metropolitan Museum Journal* 28 (1993): 169–83, and in Lovell, *Art in a Season of Revolution*, 26–27, 35–40.

16. "Autobiographical Notes of Pratt," 463–66. Pratt's own account of his adventures abroad ends with this trip to Ireland. For the subsequent period, one must refer to his son's contributions, ibid., 466–67, which begin, however, only at 1785, and to Sawitzky, *Matthew Pratt*, 29–31.

17. July 3, 1777, Collections of the Genealogical Society of Pennsylvania (hereafter cited as GSP), at HSP, vol. 174, Records of Christ Church, Philadelphia, Burials 1709–1785 (Philadelphia, 1907), p. 3268.

18. *MacPherson's Directory for the City and Suburbs of Philadelphia* (Philadelphia: Francis Bailey, 1785), 108.

19. "Autobiographical Notes of Pratt," 466–67. Sign-painting was an honorable pursuit and a skill to which Pratt had been introduced when he was his uncle James Claypoole's apprentice. Carl Bridenbaugh and Jessica Bridenbaugh, *Rebels and Gentlemen: Philadelphia in the Age of Franklin* (New York: Reynal & Hitchcock, 1942), 163–66; J. Thomas Scharf and Thompson Westcott, *History of Philadelphia, 1609–1884* (Philadelphia: L. H. Evarts & Co., 1884), 2: 984, 1034–35. For the multiple occupations of portrait painters, see Saunders and Miles, *American Colonial Portraits*, vii (foreword), 1, 19, 40, and Susan Rather, "Benjamin West's Professional Endgame and the Historical Conundrum of William Williams," *William and Mary Quarterly*, 3d Ser., 59 (2002): 828–31. Not given to praising local product or talent, the French émigré Moreau de St. Méry nevertheless thought Philadelphia artisans of the 1790s made "remarkably beautiful signboards" that were far superior to the signboards in Paris that contained "the most lamentable mistakes in language." *Moreau de St. Méry's American Journey*, trans. and ed. Kenneth Roberts and Anna M. Roberts (Garden City, NY: Doubleday & Company, 1947), 176–77.

20. "Autobiographical Notes of Pratt," 462; and see J. I. Mombert, *Authentic History of Lancaster County in the State of Pennsylvania* (Lancaster, PA: J. E. Barr & Co., 1869), 387–89; Brooke Hindle, *The Pursuit of Science in Revolutionary America, 1735–1789* (Chapel Hill: University of North Carolina Press, 1956), 309–11.

21. This portrait was acquired by the Philadelphia Museum of Art in 1972, with prior ownership documented in Elizabeth Powel's family. See Tatum, *Philadelphia Georgian*, 14–17.

22. Sawitzky, *Matthew Pratt*, 43–44 and plate 18.

23. Alan Fern, foreword in Saunders and Miles, *American Colonial Portraits*, vii.

24. Quoted in Saunders and Miles, *American Colonial Portraits*, 45, and as to the presence of Richardson's volume in West's library, see Miles, ed., *Portrait in Eighteenth-Century America*, 65.

25. An impressive cataloguing of Willing and related family portraits in historical context may be found at http://www.worcesterart.org/Collection/Early_American/Artists/wollaston/C_Willing/discussion.html, under "John Wollaston: *Charles Willing*, 1752." T. H. Breen argues that portraits of this era reflected a social process of "self-fashioning" in which they became something more than "mere transparencies, windows that provide modern viewers with direct access to the core values of a lost

colonial reality." Portraits represented, in his analysis, the result of a negotiation between painter and sitter in which the latter could scarcely be said to have deferred to the former. See his "The Meaning of 'Likeness': Portrait-Painting in an Eighteenth-Century Consumer Society," in Miles, ed., *Portrait in Eighteenth-Century America*, 39, 47.

26. *Willing Letters and Papers*, ed. Thomas Willing Balch (Philadelphia: Allen, Lane and Scott, 1922); Alexander Du Bin, *Willing Family and Collateral Lines of Carroll-Chew-Dundas-Gyles-Jackson-McCall-Moore-Parsons-Shippen* (Philadelphia: Historical Publication Society, 1941); and Burton Alva Konkle, *Thomas Willing and the First American Financial System* (Philadelphia: University of Pennsylvania Press, 1937), 2–3. Elizabeth Powel's great-nephew Joshua Francis Fisher questioned whether the regicide Simon Mayne was an ancestor the family could legitimately claim. *Recollections of Joshua Francis Fisher Written in 1864*, ed. Sophia Cadwalader (Boston: privately printed, 1929), 40.

27. Randolph Shipley Klein, *Portrait of an Early American Family: The Shippens of Pennsylvania Across Five Generations* (Philadelphia: University of Pennsylvania Press, 1975), 5–30.

28. Charles Willing to Thomas Greenough, Feb. 8, 1744, David S. Greenough Papers, Massachusetts Historical Society, Boston, MA, as quoted in the online essay "John Wollaston: *Charles Willing*" (see note 25 above). See also Klein, *Portrait of Early American Family*, 45, 75, Appendix B-5. There is very little consistency in the Willing family, broadly defined, in the use of "Ann" and "Anne" as given names.

29. Konkle, *Thomas Willing*, 21–23 (on page 22, a photograph of the Willing house on Third Street before its demolition in the mid-nineteenth century); Scharf and Westcott, *History of Philadelphia*, 1:276–77, 2:869, 882 (but caution is needed as to accuracy of dates and identifications).

30. Konkle, *Thomas Willing*, 23; Fisher, *Recollections*, 42.

31. Thomas Willing to Thomas Willing [his uncle], Dec. 6 and 20, 1754, Thomas Willing Letter Book, HSP, 48–49, 58–59. More than a century later Joshua Francis Fisher wrote sympathetically about Charles Willing's bachelor brother in England and produced copies of the playfully affectionate letters he sent to Fisher's grandmother, his niece, addressing her as "Dear Indian." *Recollections*, 60–75. Thomas Willing sent a total of twenty-six letters during the month of December 1754, including two on Christmas day. Typical of his state of mind was this message to a correspondent firm: "the Care of his Affairs & of Nine Children now devolves on me, thank God he has provided handsomely for 'em all. . . . " Thomas Willing to Messrs. Mayne Burne & Mayne, Dec. 12, 1754, Thomas Willing Letter Book, HSP, 49.

32. The story of this drama in the family was handed down among Mary Willing Byrd's descendants and is related in a memorandum of her granddaughter's, which is now in BR Box 274, 57, at the Huntington Library, San Marino, CA, as referred to in Charles Royster, *The Fabulous History of the Dismal Swamp Company: A Story of George Washington's Time* (New York: Vintage Books/Random House, 2000), 222. In substantial part, that story was confirmed in letters that Walter Stirling sent to Thomas Willing shortly after Dorothy's elopement, as those letters were transcribed in Edinburgh, Scotland, in October 1938, with the typescript copies now in the Miscellaneous Collections at HSP. These letters from Stirling also establish his acquaintance, if not friendship, with Thomas Willing before he met Willing's sister Dorothy. As for the Stirling clan, see Thomas Willing Stirling, *The Stirlings of Caddo* (St. Andrews, Scotland: W. C. Henderson, Ltd., University Press, 1933), 100–104

(Appendix II). Charles Willing's reaction to the news of his daughter's clandestine marriage would have been all the more understandable if, as the Scottish family version had it, Dorothy was several months shy of her sixteenth birthday when Walter Stirling spirited her away. As a matter of fact, however, Dorothy was eighteen at the time of her marriage, having been baptized at Christ Church on August 18, 1735, when she was fifteen days old. Collections of GSP, at HSP, vol. 102, Records of Christ Church of Philadelphia, Baptisms 1709–1768 (Philadelphia, 1906), p. 185.

33. Collections of GSP, at HSP, vol. 102, Records of Christ Church, Baptisms 1709–1768, p. 293.

34. Elizabeth Powel to Maria H. Page, May 21, 1814, box 4, folder 11, PFP; see also Elizabeth Powel to Mary Byrd, Nov. 29, 1785, box 4, folder 3, PFP.

35. Konkle, *Thomas Willing*, 22–23. A later hand has inscribed on the reverse of the miniature "Miss Elizabeth Willing afterwards Mrs. [Eliza] Powel [taken at age] 17." Powel House Collections.

36. Konkle, *Thomas Willing*, 7–12. His historical prominence depending so much on his success as a merchant and then a banker, Thomas Willing's career in the law is often overlooked. He served as a justice of the Pennsylvania Provincial Supreme Court from 1767 to the Revolution, a position for which he was better qualified by training than many others who sat on the bench in the colonial and postcolonial periods.

37. For educational opportunities available to young women from established families in colonial Philadelphia, see Bridenbaugh and Bridenbaugh, *Rebels and Gentlemen*, 48–52; and Sarah E. Fatherly, " 'The Sweet Recourse of Reason': Elite Women's Education in Colonial Philadelphia," PMHB 128 (2004): 229–56. Joshua Francis Fisher speculates on the education his grandmother and her sisters may have received. *Recollections*, 43, 47–48.

38. Her son Charles, aged five weeks, and Ann Willing were both baptized on July 6, 1738. Collections of GSP, vol. 102, Records of Christ Church, Baptisms 1709–1768, pp. 227–28.

39. Elizabeth Powel to Mrs. [William] Fitzhugh, July 1786 (docketed as a retained copy), File No. A 543.4, Martha Washington Papers, Mount Vernon Library, Mount Vernon Ladies' Association, Mount Vernon, VA (hereafter cited as MVLA). These enlightened views about female education may correspond with a subtle change that occurred in the post-Revolutionary period. The educated woman then became the model of the republican mother and wife, providing in the new nation essential support to her family, and especially to her husband and sons. See Linda K. Kerber, *Women of the Republic: Intellect and Ideology in Revolutionary America* (Chapel Hill: University of North Carolina Press, 1980), 227–31. Such utilitarian justification for educating women is found in Benjamin Rush's *Thoughts Upon Female Education . . . Addressed to the Visitors of the Young Ladies' Academy in Philadelphia, 28 July, 1787* (Philadelphia: Prichard & Hall, 1787), which the author dedicated to Elizabeth Powel in the hope that the opinions he expressed, "so contrary to general prejudice and fashion," might cause less offense if he obtained "the patronage of a respectable and popular name." Ibid., 3.

40. Fisher, *Recollections*, 86–87, 144.

41. Milton E. Flower, *John Dickinson, Conservative Revolutionary* (Charlottesville: University Press of Virginia, 1983), 63–72, 147–67; Konkle, *Thomas Willing*, 71–79.

42. Elizabeth Willing to Mary Byrd, Aug. 15, 1768, box 4, folder 3, PFP.

43. Elizabeth Powel to Mary Byrd, Nov. 29, 1785, box 4, folder 3, PFP. Whether women were so "totally unfit" in political discourse or patriotic commitment during

the Revolutionary era or thereafter is a different matter. See Kerber, *Women of the Republic*, 69–113.

44. Aug. 7, 1769, Collections of GSP, at HSP, vol. 179, Records of Christ Church, Philadelphia, Marriages 1709–1800 (Philadelphia, 1907), p. 4349.

45. Tatum, *Philadelphia Georgian*, 6–9; Diaries of Deborah Norris Logan, vol. 12, p. 262.

46. Tatum, *Philadelphia Georgian*, 10–14; Whitfield J. Bell, Jr., *Patriot-Improvers: Biographical Sketches of Members of the American Philosophical Society* (Philadelphia: American Philosophical Society, 1997), 1:259–64, 329–30; John W. Jordan, ed., *Colonial and Revolutionary Families of Philadelphia* (New York: Lewis Publishing Company, 1911) 1:110–13; and *A Journal of Samuel Powel*, ed. Sarah Jackson (Florence: Studio Per Edizioni Scelte, 2001), 19–34 (editor's introductory essay).

47. Minutes, Philadelphia Monthly Meeting, Feb. 26, 1768, pp. 222–23 (accessible on microfilm at the Friends Historical Library, Swarthmore College, Swarthmore, PA). One has the impression that in 1760 someone other than Samuel Powel sought on his behalf a traveling certificate, or a certificate of good standing, directed to Friends abroad, and did this after Powel had departed in order to regularize his status—the application being "for a Certificate for Sam'l Powel lately embarked on a Voyage to Great Britain." Minutes, Philadelphia Monthly Meeting, Nov. 13 (adjourned meeting) and 28, 1760, pp. 293 and 295. As for John Morgan's conversion, acting under the irresistible persuasion of his fiancée, see Whitfield J. Bell, Jr., *John Morgan, Continental Doctor* (Philadelphia: University of Pennsylvania Press, 1965), 63–64.

48. Tatum, *Philadelphia Georgian*, 4–6.

49. Ibid., 46–55, 87–99; Roger W. Moss, *Historic Houses of Philadelphia: A Tour of the Region's Museum Homes* (Philadelphia: University of Pennsylvania Press, 1998), 34–39; and Nicholas B. Wainwright, *Colonial Grandeur in Philadelphia: The House and Furniture of General John Cadwalader* (Philadelphia: Historical Society of Pennsylvania, 1964), 88–101. Robert Smith, master builder and proto-architect in colonial Philadelphia, was in contractual relationship with Samuel Powel as early as 1760, resuming that relationship upon Powel's return from abroad seven years later. It is possible that Smith supervised for Charles Stedman the construction of the house on Third Street. It is even more likely that, once title passed, he took charge of the improvements that the Powels commissioned for their new house. See Charles E. Peterson (with Constance M. Greiff and Maria M. Thompson), *Robert Smith: Architect, Builder, Patriot, 1722–1777* (Philadelphia: Athenaeum of Philadelphia, 2000), 107–112.

50. Quoted in Edgar L. Pennington, "The Work of the Bray Associates in Pennsylvania," PMHB 58 (1934): 21.

51. These several interests of Samuel Powel may be observed in his "Accounts and Memoranda (property) (1786–1796)," Collections of the Library Company of Philadelphia (hereafter cited as LCP), on deposit at HSP. Fastidious bookkeeping would appear to have been an inherited trait, as substantiated for the three successive Samuel Powels. For this Samuel Powel's multiple organizational affiliations and civic responsibilities, see Bell, *Patriot-Improvers*, 1:257–59, 265–68.

52. *Diary and Autobiography of John Adams*, ed. L. H. Butterfield (Cambridge: Harvard University Press, 1961), 127; see also John Adams to Abigail Adams, Sept. 29, 1774, *Adams Family Correspondence*, ed. L. H. Butterfield (Cambridge: Harvard University Press, 1963) 1:63–64.

53. On the subject of the Chew household and the servants employed there, see Nancy E. Richards's excellent unpublished work, available through Cliveden of the

National Trust, Inc., "The City Home of Benjamin Chew, Sr., and His Family: A Case Study of the Texture of Life" (Philadelphia, 1996), pp. 27–44.

54. Apr. 19, 1770, Collections of GSP, at HSP, vol. 179, Records of Christ Church, Philadelphia 1709–1800, p. 4354; Oct. 9 and 26, 1773, Samuel Powel Receipt Book, Collections of LCP, at HSP, Mar. 1773–Dec. 1774, box 1, folder 6; Eighteen Penny Provincial Tax, 1774, Dock Ward, p. 15, on microfilm at HSP; and *Heads of Families at the First Census of the United States Taken in the Year 1790—Pennsylvania* (Washington, DC: Government Printing Office, 1908), 328.

55. Elizabeth Powel to Mrs. Alexander Wilcocks, Jan. 8, 1781, box 4, folder 3, PFP. A more satisfactory exchange of servants occurred a short time afterwards when Mrs. Shewell relinquished any claim to Sally Brown, whom she had employed as a cook but whom Elizabeth Powel planned to employ as a housemaid and laundress. Elizabeth Powel to Mrs. Shewell, and latter's endorsed reply, Aug. 27, 1782, box 3, folder 8, PFP.

56. John F. Watson, *Annals of Philadelphia, Being a Collection of Memoirs, Anecdotes & Incidents of the City and its Inhabitants From the Days of the Pilgrim Founders* (Philadelphia: E. L. Carey & A. Hart, 1830), 483. A framed photocopy of Elizabeth Powel's 1795 will is available at the Powel House. Fanny More, one of these two free black women whom Elizabeth Powel remembered in her will, may have been her husband's former slave, the "Fanny" who was married in a Christ Church ceremony in 1770.

57. The allocation of space between areas intended for entertaining and those reserved for child-rearing in colonial America is considered with particular reference to the Powel House in Richard L. Bushman, "American High-Style and Vernacular Cultures," Jack P. Greene and J. R. Pole, eds., *Colonial British America: Essays in the New History of the Early Modern Era* (Baltimore: Johns Hopkins Press, 1984), 351–52.

58. The first son was baptized on July 27, 1770, and buried on July 14, 1771. The second son was buried on July 12, 1775 (his baptism having been recorded in error, it would seem, as occurring on July 16, 1775). Collections of GSP, at HSP, vol. 167, Records of Christ Church, Philadelphia, Baptisms 1769–1794 (Philadelphia, 1906), pp. 719, 864; and Collections of GSP, at HSP, vol. 174, Records of Christ Church, Philadelphia, Burials 1709–1785 (Philadelphia, 1907), pp. 8187, 3239; and Clark, comp., *Records of Inscriptions*, 128. The child's cart or wagon, referred to in Tatum, *Philadelphia Georgian*, 134, was given to the Powel House by Mrs. Harford Willing Hare Powel.

59. June 1, 1773, Samuel Powel Receipt Book, Mar. 1773–Dec. 1774, box 1, folder 6. For Shippen's credentials as a competent obstetrician in the colonial and postcolonial period, see Klein, *Early American Family*, 112–16, 121–23; Cecil K. Drinker, *Not So Long Ago: A Chronicle of Medicine and Doctors in Colonial Philadelphia* (New York: Oxford University Press, 1937), 50–51. Drinker makes the point that midwives were usually in charge of childbirth and that male physicians were called in only as a last resort, the profession of *accoucheur* being generally thought unbecoming a gentleman; he also provides a schedule of fees that physicians were accustomed to charge in that period for their services. Ibid., 145–46.

60. Diaries of Deborah Norris Logan, vol. 12, p. 263.

61. Klein, *Early American Family*, 123–25, 192–94; Bell, *Patriot-Improvers*, 1:327–35.

62. Mar. 10, 1775, Samuel Powel Receipt Book, Jan. 15, 1773–Aug. 2, 1776, box 1, folder 7. At effusive length, Morgan dedicated to Samuel Powel, his friend and

recent traveling companion, his proposal for establishing medical schools, which was published shortly after Morgan's return to Philadelphia and which gained him precedence over Shippen. *A Discourse upon the Institution of Medical Schools in America* (Philadelphia: William Bradford, 1765), iii–vii (dedication). In that proposal he distinguished clearly between his role as physician and that of surgeon, reserving, however, the possibility of inoculating for smallpox, "where my patients or their friends object to employ another hand to make the incision." Ibid., ii (introduction). As director general of the hospitals and physician-in-chief of the Continental Army, Morgan also authored *Recommendation of Inoculation, According to Baron Dimsdale's Method* (Boston: J. Gill, 1776), in which he argued (p. 15) that, "instead of considering it a crime to inoculate, people would accuse themselves of being accessory to the death of such as fell a sacrifice to the natural small-pox, if, by their neglect the operation had been omitted." A far from risk-free operation at any age, inoculating the very young was common before Jenner's observations and the consequent adoption of vaccination. Drinker, *Not So Long Ago*, 91–100. Smallpox repeatedly approached epidemic levels in Philadelphia in the years prior to the Revolution. See Elizabeth A. Fenn, *Pox Americana: The Great Smallpox Epidemic of 1775–80* (New York: Hill and Wang, 2000), 29, 41–42.

63. Undated poem in Elizabeth Powel's handwriting, Powel House Collections. Laurie Switzer, a former manager of the Powel House, kindly called the author's attention to the existence of this poem and its location in an unexpected place at the Powel House.

64. Powel also took office in 1789 as the first mayor serving after the city government was reorganized under a new charter. Bell, *Patriot-Improvers*, 1:265–68. Bell is circumspect about attributing patriotic fervor to Powel, who "took his stand with the rebels slowly, deliberately, and doubtless with some distaste for their company." For the "Patriot Mayor" identification, see Robert C. Moon, *The Morris Family of Philadelphia: Descendants of Anthony Morris, 1654–1721* (Philadelphia: privately printed, 1898), 2:480, which affixes this title to Powel "in Revolutionary times"; Tatum, *Philadelphia Georgian*, 22, where it is reported rather than adopted; and the conclusion of the editor-compiler of the Martha Washington Papers that Powel was "a strong supporter of the Revolution," in *"Worthy Partner": The Papers of Martha Washington*, comp. Joseph E. Fields (Westport, CT: Greenwood Press, 1994), xxxvii. J. H. Powell in his *Bring Out Your Dead: The Great Plague of Yellow Fever in Philadelphia in 1793* (Philadelphia: University of Pennsylvania Press, 1949), 196, goes over the top in labeling Powel a "sterling patriot."

65. Page Smith, *James Wilson: Founding Father, 1742–1798* (Chapel Hill: University of North Carolina Press, 1956), 118–39; Konkle, *Thomas Willing*, 80–83; Burton Alva Konkle, *Benjamin Chew, 1722–1810* (Philadelphia: University of Pennsylvania Press, 1932), 145–63, 175–90.

66. Carl Van Doren, *Secret History of the American Revolution* (New York: Viking Press, 1941), 91–96. The claim that the Powels were displaced for a longer period during the British occupation figures repeatedly in current mythology. See, for example, Russell F. Weigley, ed., *Philadelphia: A 300-Year History* (New York: W. W. Norton & Company, 1982), 140; and, by necessary implication, in Bell, *Patriot-Improvers*, 1:266.

67. Earl of Carlisle to George Selwyn, June 10, [1778], in Moon, *Morris Family*, 2:481–82.

68. Elizabeth Powel to Anne Willing Francis, Apr. 2, 1778, box 4, folder 3, PFP. Arrested by the British when they occupied Philadelphia, Tench Francis, Jr., was released after the Battle of Germantown and permitted to go to his farm located near the Delaware River, in what is now West Deptford Township, Gloucester County, New Jersey. "The Barn on Paradise Farm," *Bulletin of the Gloucester County Historical Society*, vol. 7, no. 3 (March 1960). In the fall of 1777 Samuel Powel laid in cords of hickory and oak to keep the fires raging in the house on Third Street during the winter months of the British occupation. Samuel Powel Receipt Book, 1776–1778, Winterthur Museum, Garden, and Library (Collection 232), Winterthur, DE, pp. 36–38.

69. For a comprehensive biographical essay on Chastellux and his career, see the introduction of Howard C. Rice, Jr., to *Travels in North America*, 1:1–41, and as to the quoted material in the text, see ibid., 1:130, 131. An alternative translation of "until now" for the French "*jusqu'ici*" may sharpen the ambiguity that Chastellux attributed to Powel's patriotic commitment. See *Voyages de M. le Marquis de Chastellux Dans l'Amérique Septentrionale Dans les années 1780, 1781 & 1782* (Paris: Chez Prault, 1786), 1:155.

70. *Travels in North America*, 1:136 and 302 n. 30. As of his encounter of them in December 1780, Chastellux described the marriage of Samuel and Elizabeth Powel as the "happiest union . . . [of] two friends, unusually well matched in understanding, taste, and knowledge," which had lasted, in his generous calculation, for twenty years.

71. For the French salon culture and its translation to the American scene, see Susan Branson, *These Fiery Frenchified Dames: Women and Political Culture in Early National Philadelphia* (Philadelphia: University of Pennsylvania Press, 2001), 125–26, 132–38; David S. Shields, *Civil Tongues and Polite Letters in British America* (Chapel Hill: University of North Carolina Press, 1997), 99–140; Howard Mumford Jones, *America and French Culture, 1750–1848* (Chapel Hill: University of North Carolina Press, 1927), 237–40; and Anne Hollingsworth Wharton, *Salons, Colonial and Republican* (Philadelphia: J. B. Lippincott Company, 1900), 132–55.

72. See Branson, *Frenchified Dames*, 127; and Fatherly, " 'Sweet Recourse of Reason,' " 249–51.

73. Royster, *Fabulous History of Dismal Swamp Company*, 222–24, 234–36. Though acknowledging his death a tragedy, no one in the family was prepared, at least in correspondence, to admit that he died by his own hand.

74. Elizabeth Powel to [Mary Byrd], Dec. 1783, box 4, folder 3, PFP. On Lord Chesterfield's influence, both for good and for bad, see C. Dallett Hemphill, "Middle Class Rising in Revolutionary America: The Evidence from Manners," *Journal of Social History* 30 (Winter 1996), 317–44; and Bushman, "American High Style," 352–55. Elizabeth Powel would have been less inclined to praise *The Economy of Human Life*, first published in London in 1750 and then republished in many successive editions in Britain and America, had she realized that, instead of Robert Dodsley, to whom his small volume of edifying instruction was generally credited, the author of a substantial part was none other than Lord Chesterfield, Philip Dormer Stanhope. See *The Dictionary of National Biography*, s.v. "Robert Dodsley" and "Philip Dormer Stanhope."

75. Elizabeth Powel to [Mrs. Page], n.d. [1784], box 5, folder 4, PFP. From a passing reference in the letter to Congress's then sitting in Trenton, the letter was probably written late in 1784. An uncharitable great-nephew on his wife's side, born years after Samuel Powel died, dismissed him as "a conceited priggish man, & precise & peremptory as a husband." Fisher, *Recollections*, 208. That there may, however, be

more than a kernel of truth in that characterization can be read between the lines in this letter from his wife.

76. Jacob Duché to George Washington, Oct. 8, 1777, *The Papers of George Washington (Revolutionary War Series)*, ed. Philander D. Chase (Charlottesville: University Press of Virginia, 2001), 11:430–36. As early as 1763, while he was abroad, Samuel Powel wrote a friend, "I hear Duché is turned Methodist or something like it—is it true?" Samuel Powel to George Roberts, "Powel-Roberts Correspondence, 1761–1765," PMHB 18 (1894): 37. Benjamin Rush captures Duché in all his quirkiness, writing that, especially in his later years, Duché "sometimes laughed and cried alternately all day" and that, even in his heyday, "he was obliged . . . to pinch himself in the pulpit to prevent his laughing when he was preaching." *The Autobiography of Benjamin Rush: His "Travels through Life" together with his Commonplace Book for 1789–1813*, ed. George W. Corner (Princeton: Princeton University Press, 1948), 240.

77. Jacob Duché to George Washington, Apr. 2, 1783, in *The Writings of George Washington*, ed. Jared Sparks (New York: Harper & Brothers, 1847), 5:481–82 (with Washington's reply of Aug. 10, 1783), and in George Washington Papers at the American Memory Web site of the Library of Congress (see note 7 above).

78. Elizabeth Powel to Jacob Duché, n.d. [1783], box 4, folder 3, PFP; Elizabeth Powel to Martha Washington, Jan. 7, 1798, Martha Washington Papers, MVLA, in *"Worthy Partner,"* 313. William White, however, bore his predecessor no grudge and sought Duché out when White went to England to be consecrated as bishop. Bird Wilson, *Memoir of the Life of the Right Reverend William White, D. D., Bishop of the Protestant Episcopal Church in the State of Pennsylvania* (Philadelphia: James Kay, Jun. & Brother, 1839), 58.

79. Smith, *James Wilson*, 170, 389; George Lee Haskins and Herbert A. Johnson, *Foundations of Power: John Marshall, 1801–15*, vol. 2, *History of the Supreme Court of the United States* (New York: Macmillan Publishing Co, 1981), 96–100.

80. The gift to "Judge" Washington may be found on page 15 of Elizabeth Powel's last will and testament, as identified in note 139 below.

81. Elizabeth Powel to [Bushrod Washington], June 22, 1785, box 4, folder 3, PFP. In 1812, when her former protégé was Justice Washington of the United States Supreme Court, she would remind him of the pains she had taken to instill in his mind correct sentiments, "in place of those deistical opinions that had been infused into it, by your juvenile Associates." Elizabeth Powel to Judge Washington, Apr. 12, 1812, box 4, folder 8, PFP.

82. Anne Francis to Mary Byrd, Mar. 19, 1808, *Virginia Magazine of History and Biography*, 54 (1946): 117. For the cautionary precept, see Nicole Pohl and Betty A. Schellenberg, *Reconsidering the Bluestockings* (San Marino, CA: Huntington Library, 2003), 67–68; and generally Benedetta Craveri, *The Age of Conversation*, trans. Teresa Waugh (New York: New York Review of Books, 2005). As additional evidence of her political activism, Elizabeth Powel used her influence with Secretary of State Timothy Pickering to secure for her nephew Charles Willing Byrd his appointment as secretary of the Northwest Territory and may thereafter have been responsible for this nephew's becoming a federal judge in Ohio. See Elizabeth Powel to Charles Willing Byrd, Feb. 28, 1800, the Lilly Library, Indiana University, Bloomington.

83. Walter Isaacson, *Benjamin Franklin: An American Life* (New York: Simon & Schuster, 2003), 459.

84. Elizabeth Powel to Miss Martha Hare, May 21, 1814, box 4, folder 11, PFP.

85. It does not appear from Washington's diary entries that he was a guest of the Powels during this period, although he accepted invitations from two of their immediate neighbors on Third Street: Benjamin Chew (Sept. 22) and Thomas Willing (Sept. 24 and Oct. 19). *The Diaries of George Washington*, eds. Donald Jackson and Dorothy Twohig (Charlottesville: University Press of Virginia, 1978), 3:274–87. Benjamin Franklin's daughter, Sarah Bache, writing to her father in Paris on January 17, 1779, provides the first evidence of the Washingtons as guests at the Powel House when she reports to her father that she danced there with General Washington on Benjamin Franklin's birthday, which her dancing partner confided was also his and his wife's twentieth wedding anniversary. *The Papers of Benjamin Franklin*, ed. Barbara B. Oberg et al. (New Haven: Yale University Press, 1990), 28:391 and n. 4 (explaining an apparent discrepancy arising from the coincidence of Franklin's birth date of January 6 under the Julian calendar with the Washingtons' wedding anniversary under the Gregorian one; the party must, therefore, have taken place on January 6, 1779).

86. See *"Worthy Partner,"* xxxi–xxxii (introduction).

87. *The Diaries of George Washington*, 5:191, 192, 211, 212 (for the Powels' trip to Mount Vernon); for the somewhat equivocal relationship between Washington and Elizabeth Powel, see Flexner, *George Washington and the New Nation*, 313–21, and Flexner, *George Washington: Anguish and Farewell (1793–1799)* (Boston: Little, Brown and Company, 1972), 344–46.

88. Elizabeth Powel to [George Washington], Nov. 17, 1792, in *The Papers of George Washington (Presidential Series)*, ed. Christine Steinberg Patrick (Charlottesville: University Press of Virginia, 2002), 11:395–97, where it is noted that Mount Vernon has a draft of the letter docketed in the hand of Elizabeth Powel under date of Nov. 4, 1792, which suggests an earlier date for their meeting than the autograph letter would indicate. For the boldness of this communication, see Richard Norton Smith, *Patriarch: George Washington and the New American Nation* (New York: Houghton Mifflin Company, 1993), 150–51.

89. Douglas Southall Freeman, *George Washington: A Biography* (New York: Charles Scribner's Sons, 1954), 6:378–84 (the remark to Jefferson on p. 383).

90. George and Martha Washington to Elizabeth Powel, Feb. 21, 1793, Martha Washington Papers, MVLA, in *"Worthy Partner,"* 245.

91. *The Diary of Samuel Breck 1827–1833*, PMHB 103 (1979): 234.

92. Fisher, *Recollections*, 206. Often careless about names, places, and dates, and never hesitating to express an opinion, Joshua Francis Fisher was wrong in identifying Barbé-Marbois as Elizabeth Powel's partner in the opening dance. Barbé-Marbois's main claim to fame would be negotiating for France the sale of the Louisiana territory. He left Philadelphia and America in 1785, never to return. François, Marquis de Barbé-Marbois, *Our Revolutionary Forefathers*, ed. and trans. Eugene Parker Chase (New York: Duffield & Co., 1929), 18–28 (introduction).

93. "Mr. Hill's Verses a little altered by [some] Friends of his," n.d., box 7, folder 6, PFP. Henry Hill had turned sixty years of age the prior September. This particular folder contains two other versions of his birthday tribute to Elizabeth Powel, which, for propriety's sake, seems to have required editing. Very similar verses that James Bowdoin II was inspired to compose in praise of his wife provide "a good sense of the erotic focus of the eighteenth century male gaze." Margaretta M. Lovell, "Painters and Their Customers: Aspects of Art and Money in Eighteenth-Century America," in *Of Consuming Interests: The Style of Life in the Eighteenth Century*, ed. Cary Carson, Ronald Hoffman, and Peter J. Albert, (Charlottesville: University Press of

Virginia, 1994), 300–301. For more about Henry Hill, see David W. Maxey, "Madeira, Quakerism, and Rebellion: Reviving Henry Hill," 93 *Quaker History* (Fall 2004): 47–75.

94. Powell, *Bring Out Your Dead*, 1–2, 18–28, 64–69; Martin S. Pernick, "Politics, Parties, and Pestilence: Epidemic Yellow Fever in Philadelphia and the Rise of the First Party System," in J. Worth Estes and Billy G. Smith, eds., *A Melancholy Scene of Devastation: The Public Response to the 1793 Yellow Fever Epidemic* (Canton, MA: Science History Publications/USA, 1997), 130–34. The Drinkers were fortunate enough to have left Philadelphia for Germantown early in the summer of 1793 where they kept their distance from the city until the arrival of the first frost at the beginning of November. *The Diary of Elizabeth Drinker*, ed. Elaine Forman Crane (Boston: Northeastern University Press, 1991), 2:495–524.

95. Elizabeth Powel to George and Martha Washington, [Sept.] 9, 1793, George Washington Papers, Library of Congress, and in "*Worthy Partner*," 251–52. The original letter in the Library of Congress is dated Monday, August 9, 1793, but internally it is clear that the letter was composed and sent on the eve of the Washingtons' departure; by way of added confirmation, September 9 in that year, but not August 9, fell on a Monday.

96. Benjamin Rush to Julia Rush, Sept. 26 and 29, 1793, in *Letters of Benjamin Rush*, ed. L. H. Butterfield (Princeton: Princeton University Press, 1951), 2:685 and 686. The young doctor whose lack of resolve Rush criticized was Andrew Hall, whom Elizabeth Powel would remember in her will in "testimony of my gratitude for the affectionate attendance on my best friend." The gift to Hall was on page 2 of Elizabeth Powel's original will (see note 139 below).

97. For the provisions in Samuel Powel's will, see note 111 below, and in Elizabeth Powel's 1795 will, note 56 above.

98. Robert Morris to Elizabeth Powel, Dec. 7, 1793, box 3, folder 8, PFP.

99. Elizabeth Powel to "Sister Hare," Jan. 3, 1796, Society Small Collections, Elizabeth Willing Powel folder, HSP. On his deathbed George Washington instructed his secretary: "do not let my body be put into the vault in less than two days after I am dead." Quoted in John Alexander Carroll and Mary Wells Ashworth, *George Washington*, vol. 7 of multivolume biography by Douglas Southall Freeman (New York: Charles Scribner's Sons, 1957), 624. Elizabeth Drinker recorded the sobering experience of Samuel Shoemaker's attendant who, thinking Shoemaker dead, went out to get the coffin, only to discover upon his return that the deceased was sitting on the side of the bed, endeavoring to put his shoes on. It would have been sobering too for Samuel Shoemaker if he long survived, which he didn't. *Diary of Elizabeth Drinker* (entry of Oct. 17, 1793), 1:519.

100. Elizabeth Powel to Mr. and Mrs. Benjamin Chew, Jr., Sept. 26, 1801, Chew Family Papers (Collection 2050), HSP.

101. "Samuel Powel Accounts & Memoranda (property) (1786–1796)," LCP Collections at HSP.

102. Elizabeth Powel to Martha Washington, Christmas Day, 1797, Martha Washington Papers, MVLA, in "*Worthy Partner*," 311.

103. A. Stockton to Elizabeth Powel, June 21, 1797, box 3, folder 8, PFP. For a similar encounter, see the report of an evening's entertainment at Third Street in Roger Griswold to Matthew Griswold, May 9, 1796, William Griswold Lane Memorial Collection, Yale University Manuscripts and Archives, New Haven, CT, photostatic copy, available in typescript at the Powel House.

104. Elizabeth Powel to Rebecca Baynton, May 7, 1817, box 5, folder 3, PFP.

105. Williamina Cadwalader to Ann Ridgely, Feb. 20 (Mar. 8), 1797, in *What Them Befell: The Ridgelys of Delaware & Their Circle in Colonial & Federal Times: Letters 1751–1890*, ed. Mabel Lloyd Ridgely (Portland, ME: Anthoensen Press, 1949), 103. For Washington's last birthday celebration in Philadelphia, see Lynn Matluck Brooks, "Emblem of Gaiety, Love, and Legislation: Dance in Eighteenth-Century Philadelphia," PMHB 115 (1991): 81–82.

106. Elizabeth Powel to ________, Nov. 3, 1809, box 4, folder 5, PFP.

107. Quoted in M. G. Jones, *Hannah More* (Cambridge: Cambridge University Press, 1952), 197.

108. Elizabeth Powel to Martha Washington, Nov. 31, 1787, Martha Washington Papers, MVLA, in "*Worthy Partner*," 199. An affectation widespread in Philadelphia society between the American and French Revolutions, Elizabeth Powel's fractured French was no doubt lost on Martha Washington. Jones, *America and French Culture*, 186–200.

109. For "beloved offspring" as an emotionally charged term of reference, see Elizabeth Powel to Maria H. Page, May 21, 1814, box 4, folder 11, PFP. The quotation in *Oxford English Dictionary*, 2d ed., s.v. "Pledge," is from Sir William D'Avenant's "Gondibert." Elizabeth Powel's cited usage is in her letters to Rosalie Nelson Page, June 29, 1814, box 4, folder 11, and to Thomas Mayne Willing, Apr. 21, 1815, box 5, folder 1, PFP; and in Memorandum of Elizabeth Powel, Apr. 13, 1813, box 5, folder 7, PFP; it also appears in Elizabeth Powel to Mrs. William Meredith, Oct. 25, 1815, box 5, folder 1, PFP.

110. The statement in the text, though presently correct, must be qualified: Samuel Powel's Ledger Book, covering the period 1760–1793, in the LCP Collections at HSP, has been misplaced. It cannot therefore be completely ruled out that, if and when found, the ledger book may contain an entry for the Pratt portrait.

111. Samuel Powel's will was probated in Philadelphia on Nov. 11, 1793, as No. 336 of 1793. The original document consisting of two pages is in the Philadelphia City Archives at 3101 Market Street (hereafter cited as PCA). The will also was recorded in the Office of the Register of Wills, Philadelphia, in Will Book W, p. 569 et seq. For the grand federal procession and Powel's participation, see Scharf & Westcott, *History of Philadelphia*, 1:447–52.

112. Elizabeth Powel to Mrs. [William] Fitzhugh, July 1786, Martha Washington Papers, MVLA (see note 39 above). This may be the letter that Elizabeth Powel, in a postscript she added to her husband's letter, asked the Washingtons to forward to Mrs. Fitzhugh. Samuel Powel (and Elizabeth Powel) to George Washington, Aug. 21, 1786, *The Papers of George Washington (Confederation Series)*, ed. W. W. Abbot and Dorothy Twohig (Charlottesville: University Press of Virginia, 1995), 4:226–27.

113. See John Hare Powel, "Memorandum for my Children, Newport, Rhode Island, Aug. 28, 1851," in Robert Johnston Hare-Powel, "Hare-Powel and Kindred Families: A Record" (1907, but thereafter supplemented), in typescript at HSP and the Powel House; lacking consecutive pagination throughout, this valuable family memoir may be found in draft form in the several folders in box 43, PFP. His aunt confirmed his account that she had nursed him "in a dangerous putrid Fever, and sore Throat, evidently at the hazard of my life." Memorandum of Elizabeth Powel, Apr. 13, 1813, box 5, folder 7, PFP.

114. Robert Hare to Richard Hare, Sept. 1, 1808, box 7, folder 7, PFP. Elizabeth Powel's requirement that her favorite nephew assume the name of John Powel as a

condition to inheriting from her first appears in her 1795 will. As to her covering the entire cost of his trip abroad, see Memorandum of Elizabeth Powel, Apr. 13, 1813, box 5, folder 7, PFP.

115. The legislature authorized the name change by special legislation approved on Jan. 18, 1808. *The Statutes at Large of Pennsylvania from 1806 to 1809*, vol. 18 (Harrisburg, PA: William Stanley Ray, State Printer, 1915), 710. John Hare Powel apparently was not baptized until July 12, 1814, at the age of twenty-eight, and then under his transposed name. Collections of GSP, at HSP, vol. 167, Records of Christ Church of Philadelphia, Baptisms 1794–1819 (Philadelphia, 1906), p. 1951. His continuing identification with his parents is set out in "Memorandum for my Children," in Hare-Powel, "Hare-Powel and Kindred Families," and in the provisions of his mother's will, executed on Feb. 8, 1812, and probated on Dec. 22, 1818, two years after Margaret Hare's death, under File No. 4 of 1819, Philadelphia Register of Wills, as recorded in Will Book 6, page 625 et seq. For the history of American adoption law, see Laurence M. Friedman, *A History of American Law*, 2d ed. (New York: Simon & Schuster, 1985), 211–12.

116. Edgar P. Richardson, "James Claypoole, Junior, Re-discovered," *Art Quarterly*, 33 (1970): 161, 174 n. 8; Saunders and Miles, *American Colonial Portraits*, 311–13. According to Nancy Schrom Dye and Daniel Blake Smith, in "Mother Love and Infant Death," 330–38, it was only toward the end of the eighteenth century that concepts of mothering had changed to the point that women reacted with sharp intensity to losing their infant children in death, a development that would appear simultaneously reflected in the more frequent painting of family portraits. See Lovell, *Art in a Season of Revolution*, 141–63.

117. There is admitted risk in attempting to determine a subject's age by the way she looks in a portrait. In Pratt's portrayal of her, Elizabeth Powel appears to have entered the spacious range of middle age—in her forties perhaps but not yet fifty. In December 1790, Abigail Adams sang Elizabeth Powel's praises as "a very interesting woman," while describing her as "motherly" and having "turned of fifty." Quoted in Flexner, *George Washington and the New Nation*, 314.

118. Elizabeth Powel to [Anne Willing Francis], Apr. 2, 1778, box 4, folder 3, PFP.

119. Sawitzky, *Matthew Pratt*, 79–80 (plate 25). Ann Shippen Willing had sat for her portrait by Robert Feke in 1746. It is now in the collections of the Winterthur Museum. See Edgar P. Richardson, *American Paintings and Related Pictures in The Henry Francis du Pont Winterthur Museum* (Charlottesville: University Press of Virginia, 1986), 28–29.

120. Charles Willson Peale painted five portraits of members of the Cadwalader family in the 1770–1772 period; all five portraits now hang in the Powel Room at the Philadelphia Museum of Art. See Wainwright, *Colonial Grandeur in Philadelphia*, 45–47, 108–15; Darrel Sewell, "Charles Willson Peale's Portraits of the Cadwalader Family," in Jack L. Lindsay and Darrel Sewell, *The Cadwalader Family: Art and Style in Early Philadelphia* (*Philadelphia Museum of Art Bulletin*, vol. 91, nos. 384–85, Fall 1996), 24–31. See also, for Pratt's circumstances, "Autobiographical Notes of Pratt," 466–67; and, for the infrequency of repeat commissions, Lovell, *Art in a Season of Revolution*, 13. According to Joshua Francis Fisher, Ann Willing's son Thomas, "not prodigal of attentions to the poor old lady," forced her to leave the family house on Third Street and to take up residence, with her daughters Abigail and Margaret, in a more modest dwelling on Pine Street between Front and Second, where, as

"gentlewoman," she is listed in the directories for 1785 and for 1791, the latter being the year of her death. *Recollections*, 86–87; *The Philadelphia Directory* (Philadelphia: Young Steward, and M'Culloch, 1785), 81, and *The Philadelphia Directory*, comp. Clement Biddle (Philadelphia: James & Johnson, 1791), 142.

121. Reinhardt, " 'The Work of Fancy and Taste,' " 4–18. In an idealized treatment of dress, "portrait painters had more in common with dressmakers than they would have liked to admit." Ibid., 15.

122. Sawitzky, *Matthew Pratt*, 40–41 (plate 23) [Mrs. William Bradford, Jr.]; 42–43 (plate 28) [Mrs. John Bush]; and 78–79 (plate 5) [Mrs. Benjamin West]. For a recent examination of the companion portraits of Mrs. John Bush and her husband, both by Pratt, see Lauren B. Hewes, *Portraits in the Collection of the American Antiquarian Society* (Worcester, MA: American Antiquarian Society, 2004), 95–97; the outside date for the portrait of Mrs. John Bush has to be 1788, the year of her death.

123. Thomas Jefferson to Martha Jefferson, Dec. 22, 1783, *The Papers of Thomas Jefferson*, ed. Julian P. Boyd et al. (Princeton: Princeton University Press, 1952), 6:417.

124. " 'The Work of Fancy and Taste,' " 4, 12. See also Aileen Ribeiro, " 'The Whole of Dress': Costume in the Work of John Singleton Copley," in Rebora and Saiti et al., eds., *John Singleton Copley in America*, 105–110; and Lovell, *Art in a Season of Revolution*, 49–93, where the author makes a convincing case that a blue dress of rococo intricacies appearing in three successive Copley portraits was an actual "itinerant" garment, replicated with the consent of the three women whom he painted. As a rare example of "invented" male costume, a great-aunt of Samuel Powel's, scandalized when she saw a miniature of Samuel Powel sent from Britain in which he appeared decked out in gaudy un-Quakerish clothes, was reassured by her daughter: "O mother . . . it's the way of the Painters to make Pictures look fine." Samuel Morris to Samuel Powel, Mar. 9, 1765, in Moon, *Morris Family*, 2:473.

125. Elizabeth Powel to Mrs. William Meredith, Oct. 1, 1813, box 4, folder 10, PFP. See also Elizabeth Powel to [Benjamin Trott], Feb. 3, 1809, box 4, folder 5, PFP, in which she thanked Trott for producing a miniature, presumably of her, "with great taste," although she felt compelled to add that it might be "a too flattering likeness to be a perfectly correct one." Perhaps in reliance on this Trott miniature, Thomas Sully is said to have later painted a heroic portrait of Elizabeth Powel. Tatum, *Philadelphia Georgian*, 154 n. 90.

126. Lovell, *Art in a Season of Revolution*, 10–11.

127. Tatum, *Philadelphia Georgian*, 24–25; Fisher, *Recollections*, 209; Scharf & Westcott, *History of Philadelphia*, 2:994; *The Philadelphia Directory, City and County Register, for 1802*, comp. James Robinson (Philadelphia: William W. Woodward, 1802), 195 (Elizabeth Powel, widow, at 152 Chestnut Street). Later identified as 207 Chestnut Street, the three-story brick house and the detached two-story brick stable located in the rear were surveyed in 1818 for insurance purposes. See Policy Nos. 3936 and 3937, Mutual Assurance Company for Insuring Houses for Loss by Fire, HSP. Deborah Logan wrote that Elizabeth Powel was responsible for building the Chestnut Street house. Diaries of Deborah Norris Logan, vol. 12, unnumbered pages inserted at end of volume (entry for Feb. 23, 1830). The property forming the building site consisted of two contiguous lots fronting on Chestnut Street and having equivalent areas, conveyed to Elizabeth Powel by separate deeds each dated Mar. 27, 1802, as follows: from John and Hannah Moore (for a consideration of twenty-three hundred

dollars) and from David Evans (for a consideration of twenty-two hundred dollars), as recorded on Apr. 6, 1802, in the Office of the Recorder of Deeds, Philadelphia, in Deed Book EF 9, p. 97, and Deed Book EF 9, p. 98, respectively.

128. Elizabeth Powel to Thomas M. Willing, Jan. 14, 1808, box 4, folder 4, PFP; Elizabeth Powel to John H. Powel, Nov. 8, 1808, box 4, folder 4, PFP. As for her retrospective view of Hamilton: "However the virulence of party spirit may have led to the execration of General Hamiltons sentiments on every subject, yet experience, and Posterity will I suspect give a verdict in favour of his political opinions." Elizabeth Powel to Mrs. Hopkinson, Feb. 13, 1816, box 5, folder 2, PFP.

129. Elizabeth Powel to Col. John Powel, Jan 30, 1815, box 5, folder 1, PFP. The day after she sent this letter, *Poulson's American Daily Advertiser*, Elizabeth Powel's preferred newspaper, carried a report from a foreign traveler to the effect that peace was imminent, but it was not until the edition of February 13 that she would have read about the peace treaty.

130. Elizabeth Powel to Mrs. David Gray, June 22, 1808, box 4, folder 4, PFP. For lesser service, she rewarded Isaac Elliott, who had made "a pretty bird for her Screen" and "pens for her use," with the New Year's gift of a penknife. Elizabeth Powel to Isaac Elliott, Jan. 6, 1812, box 4, folder 8, PFP. The legacy to Gray appears on p. 17 of her will, identified in note 139 below.

131. Elizabeth Powel to E. S. Burd, June 17, 1811, box 4, folder 7, PFP; Elizabeth Powel to James Kelly. Apr. 4, 1815, box 5, folder 2, PFP. Ennels Cork received his annuity under a codicil dated Mar. 17, 1824, p. 10, to Elizabeth Powel's will, identified in note 139 below. Robert Johnston Hare-Powel, the diligent family historian, has Ennels Cork "a former slave" dying in about 1882 "at the great age of 106." Neither his status as a former slave nor his purported age at death is supported in this record of his employment by Mrs. Powel. See "Supplement Mrs. Samuel Powel" in "Hare-Powel and Kindred Families."

132. Elizabeth Powel to Dr. Kuhn, Nov. 3, 1815, box 5, folder 1, PFP; *Diary of Elizabeth Drinker* (entry of Nov. 29, 1803), 3:1708. For the adversarial relationship between Rush and Kuhn, see Drinker, *Not So Long Ago*, 150–56.

133. As a merchant, Charles Willing imported slaves for sale; he also appears to have advertised for sale slaves of his own who were "used to all sorts of country business." *Pennsylvania Gazette*, June 25 and Nov. 26, 1747, Apr. 26, 1750. His son Thomas Willing was recorded in the provincial tax assessment of 1774 as owning one slave. Eighteen Penny Provincial Tax, 1774, Dock Ward, p. 15, on microfilm at HSP. The slave population steadily diminished in Philadelphia in the decade before the Revolution, in part because of employer preference for free or indentured white workers but also because of growing sentiment in favor of emancipation. See Gary B. Nash and Jean R. Soderlund, *Freedom by Degrees: Emancipation in Pennsylvania and Its Aftermath* (New York: Oxford University Press, 1991), 74–98. Pennsylvania's emancipation statute: "An Act for the Gradual Abolition of Slavery," passed Mar. 1, 1780, *The Statutes at Large of Pennsylvania From 1682 to 1801*, vol. 10 (Harrisburg, PA: William Stanley Ray, State Printer, 1904), 67–73.

134. Pennsylvania Abolition Society Papers, Minute Book, General Meeting, 1825–1847, vol. 3, p. 117, HSP (microfilm); Elizabeth Powel to Edward S. Burd, May 27, 1814, box 4, folder 11, PFP. The provisions in the will dated May 22, 1819, identified in note 139 below, are found on pages 19–20.

135. Elizabeth Powel to John Hare Powel, Oct. 1, 1809, box 4, folder 5, PFP. In this letter she anticipated her nephew's possible rejoinder that Samuel Powel himself

constituted a notable exception to the rule of gainful employment. "His constitution was delicate, indeed he was a Valetudinarian and had not been bred to any pecuniary Employment." But a prodigal nephew was cautioned that his uncle "did not live indolently nor spend his time in scenes of frivolous dissipation." The awkward engagement at eighteen is the subject of a separate letter from Elizabeth Powel to an inquisitive niece, Ann W. Morris, Apr. 27, 1811, box 4, folder 7, PFP.

136. Quoted in "Memorandum for my Children" in Hare-Powel, "Hare-Powel and Kindred Families." A familiar described John Hare Powel in his late years "as always the handsomest man of his time" but who "never lived happily with his wife & has few friends." *A Philadelphia Perspective: The Diary of Sidney George Fisher Covering the Years 1834–1871*, ed. Nicholas B. Wainwright (Philadelphia: Historical Society of Pennsylvania, 1967), 149, 205.

137. Elizabeth Powel's frenzied reaction to her nephew's entanglement with "the woman in Baltimore" is set forth in Elizabeth Powel to Thomas Cadwalader, Aug. 17, 1814, box 4, folder 11, PFP; Elizabeth Powel to "Miss Hare" [John Powel's sister], Aug. 5, 1814, box 4, folder 11, PFP; and Memorandum of Elizabeth Powel, Apr. 13, 1813, box 5, folder 7, PFP. For a less overwrought view of "The Three Graces" and their parents, see George C. Keidel, "Catonsville Biographies," *Maryland Historical Magazine* 16 (1921): 299–313; and *"Anywhere So Long As There be Freedom": Charles Carroll of Carrollton, His Family & His Friends* (Baltimore: Baltimore Museum of Art, 1975), 231–45.

138. Two letters of Elizabeth Powel to Bishop William White, who would be named an executor and trustee under her new will, provide evidence of the existence of prior wills: July 30, 1807, box 4, folder 3, and Dec. 13, 1816, box 5, folder 2, PFP. For a while Elizabeth Powel probably relied on both Edward Burd and his son Edward Shippen Burd for legal advice, but it was the latter who would eventually assume responsibility for the preparation of her will or wills and to whom she dictated provisions that often found their way into the final document without change.

139. Elizabeth Powel's will, together with the four codicils, was probated on Jan. 25–30, 1830, under File No. 14 of 1830, Philadelphia Register of Wills, and recorded in Will Book 9, page 422 et seq. Unfortunately, the entire will is all but illegible in the microfilm version available at HSP, and the will book in which the provisions of the will and codicils were transcribed verbatim has been either lost or misplaced in the office of the Register of Wills. Although the original documents executed by Elizabeth Powel (with the exception of one missing codicil) may be found in PCA, this material is in tattered, disintegrating condition and may not survive intact much longer.

140. Will dated May 22, 1819, PCA, pp. 5, 8, 9–10, 13, 14, 15.

141. The elaborate entail provisions, attempting to ensure male primogeniture, were buttressed by a conveyance in trust to Elizabeth Powel's executors. Ibid., pp. 34–40. As a general matter, and over a long stretch of history, both English and American law have disfavored such dynastic arrangements. See J. H. Baker, *An Introduction to English Legal History*, 3d ed. (London: Butterworths, 1990), 318–36. John Hare Powel explained his aunt's intention in "A Memorandum for my Children" in Hare-Powel, "Hare-Powel and Kindred Families." The particular residuary clause, relating to tangible personal property and located a third of the way through the will (on p. 17), reads: "All my household furniture, not otherwise herein particularly bequeathed, also my Horses and Carriages and my wines and other groceries, I give to my nephew John Hare Powel."

142. In the legislation authorizing the name change to John Hare Powel (see note 115 above), the reason for petitioning the Legislature was recited as follows: "it has been represented by John Hare Powel, son of Robert Hare of the city of Philadelphia, that at the request of a near relation, he had deemed it expedient . . . to change his name from John Powel Hare to John Hare Powel."

143. Amy Roberts's maiden name was Kennard. See Elizabeth Powel to [Edward S. Burd], June 18, 1811, box 4, folder 7, PFP. Her parents were probably Jacob Kennard and Mary Wallis, married in the First Baptist Church in Philadelphia, on Dec. 17, 1763. *Record of Pennsylvania Marriages Prior to 1810* (Baltimore: Genealogical Publishing Company, 1968), 1:755. A Jacob Kennard is listed in MacPherson's 1785 directory at 309 Arch Street (p. 74), but does not appear in directories thereafter. Amy Roberts's husband, William Roberts, died toward the end of the eighteenth century. Apparently a tailor by trade, he was the son of William Roberts, a house carpenter, and his wife, Hannah, who lived near Elizabeth Powel on Chestnut Street. See *The Philadelphia Directory*, comp. Francis White (Philadelphia: Young, Stewart, and M'Culloch, 1785), 61 (placing the older William Roberts on Chestnut Street between Sixth and Seventh Streets); and the will of William Roberts (the father) dated Nov. 14, 1806, and probated on May 16, 1808, in the office of the Register of Wills under File No. 53 of 1808, and recorded in Will Book 2, p. 296 et seq.

144. Elizabeth Powel to T. W. Francis, Nov. 27, 1800, box 3, folder 8, PFP; Elizabeth Powel to Amy Roberts, Sept. 24, 1808, box 4, folder 4, PFP.

145. Elizabeth Powel to Edward S. Burd, June 18, 1811, box 4, folder 7, PFP; Elizabeth Powel to Margaret Hare, Aug. 21, 1816, box 5, folder 2, PFP.

146. For the provisions relating to Amy and her children, see will dated May 22, 1819, pp. 3, 4, 9, 23, and 48, and the codicil dated Mar. 17, 1824, pp. 6–7. The codicil confirmed that since the date of the will, Amy Roberts's daughter Maria had married and given birth to a child who received the name of Elizabeth Powel Murphy. The one-hundred pound annuity, when converted to dollars, equaled two hundred sixty-six dollars and sixty-seven cents a year.

147. Diaries of Deborah Norris Logan, vol. 12, p. 265 and unnumbered pages inserted at the end of volume (entry for Feb. 23, 1830).

148. Schedule 2, certified as of Feb. 2, 1830, in the Inventory and Appraisement (consisting of four separate schedules), is in the will file in the Estate of Elizabeth Powel, Dec'd, PCA. The appraisers for the Schedule 2 items do not inspire complete confidence when they locate Mrs. Powel's house one block to the west of where it stood. There is a respectable body of case law to the effect that a bequest of "furniture" encompasses paintings. See, for example, Sonja A. Soehnel (Annotation), "What Passes Under Terms 'Furniture' or 'Furnishings' in Will," 21 *American Law Reports* 4th (1983), 388–90.

149. Collections of GSP, at HSP, Ronaldson Cemetery Records of Interments, vol. 2., Oct. 10, 1844, in which Amy Roberts's death, her estimated age, and burial are recorded at p. 330. Her son William died and was buried in the same cemetery plot fourteen years later. Ibid., Sept. 18, 1858, p. 334.

150. *McElroy's Philadelphia Directory for 1844* (Philadelphia: Edward C. Biddle, 1844), 228 (Murphy), 265 (Amy Roberts), and 266 (William D. Roberts).

151. Will of Amy Roberts dated July 26, 1839, and acknowledged a second time on Sept. 14, 1841, as probated on Oct. 21, 1844, under File No. 200 of 1844 in the Philadelphia Register of Wills, and recorded in Will Book 17, p. 311 et seq. The will

file at PCA contains both her will and the Inventory and Appraisement made by Peter Snyder and David Headman, which they certified under date of Nov. 5, 1844.

152. In the 1895 city directory, Lindsay was identified as a publisher, and in later directories as dealing in "pictures."

153. "Supplement Mrs. Samuel Powel" in Hare-Powel, "Hare-Powel and Kindred Families"; and "Powel House Soon to be Torn Down," *Public Ledger*, Apr. 26, 1909, and "Copley's Portrait of 'Lady Elizabeth Powel,' " *Philadelphia Record*, May 9, 1909.

154. Charles Henry Hart to editor of *American Art News*, May 20, 1912, in Charles Henry Hart, Scrapbook, 1909–1915, PAFA Archives.

155. Charles Henry Hart, "A Limner of Colonial Days," *Harper's Weekly*, July 4, 1896 (vol. 40, no. 2063), 665, and in Charles Henry Hart, Scrapbook, 1892–1907, PAFA Archives.

156. The portrait, identified as "Madam Powel," is in the collections of the Boston Museum of Fine Arts. For biographical information about Francis Alexander, see Dunlap, *History of Rise and Progress of Arts*, 2:426–33; and Franklin Kelly with Nicolai Cikovsky, Jr., Deborah Chotner and John Davis, *American Paintings of the Nineteenth Century, Part I* (Washington, DC: National Gallery of Art, 1996), 3. Alexander's presence in Philadelphia at about this time cannot be reliably established; it was, however, during this period that he was beginning to achieve recognition and command increasingly higher fees for his work.

157. Lafayette, in his triumphal return to America, visited Philadelphia twice—first in late September and early October of 1824 and then again in July 1825. Scharf and Westcott, *History of Philadelphia*, 1:608–609, 615. Elizabeth Powel was on friendly terms with Lafayette during the Revolutionary period. She queried her niece in 1784 about why her Virginia relations had not turned out en masse for the ball in Richmond honoring "the General [Washington] & Marquis Fayette. I think if I had been a young lady I shou'd have rode fifty miles to testify my Respect for such illustrious Characters." Elizabeth Powel to [Mrs. Page], n.d. [1784], box 5, folder 4, PFP. The plan to march down Chestnut Street to the State House, "passing the dwellings of Mrs. Robert Morris and Mrs. Powell, old friends of the General," was set forth in a "Memorandum of Procession," n.d., in Lafayette Reception papers at HSP (Collection AM .3651), folder 14. At the last moment the route was altered, so that, having passed before the house of Mrs. Robert Morris, when "the General rose and bowed toward the widow of his early friend," the parade left Chestnut Street and moved southward on Eighth Street. See *United States Gazette*, Sept. 30, 1824.

158. Unlike the widow of Robert Morris, Elizabeth Powel declined to attend the many grand public celebrations in Lafayette's honor. Nevertheless, it was reported on October 1, 1824, in *Poulson's American Daily Advertiser* that "the General dined at home yesterday and in the evening paid some visits to old and esteemed acquaintances." Elizabeth Powel left the considerable lace she owned to her niece Julia Powel. Will dated May 22, 1819, PCA, p. 4.

159. Elizabeth Powel to Thomas Willing, Feb. 22, 1815, box 5, folder 1, PFP.

Index

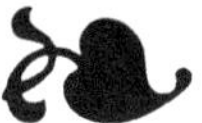

www.ingramcontent.com/pod-product-compliance
Lightning Source LLC
LaVergne TN
LVHW081601100826
845153LV00004B/430

* 9 7 8 0 8 7 1 6 9 9 6 4 0 *